Teaching with a Strength-Based Approach

Helping students improve doesn't have to mean remediating their deficits. In this important book, Steven Baron shows the benefits of a strength-based approach that instead emphasizes students' assets and capabilities, making them feel more connected to teachers and peers and more engaged in learning.

You'll learn practical, research-backed ways to help students of all grade levels identify and celebrate their strengths, develop self-confidence and a growth mindset, build intrinsic motivation, overcome a fear of making mistakes, manage their feelings, focus on gratitude, and more. You'll also discover ways to create a more strength-based Individual Education Plan (IEP), increase your own resilience as a teacher, and build a strength-based culture throughout your school and district.

The appendix provides a variety of exercises you can use to help students focus on their strengths, foster kindness, and understand the impact of bullying. Students spend approximately 1300 hours during the year with teachers; this resource will help you make this time as affirming as possible so students are ready to learn and grow.

Steven Baron served as a school psychologist at the elementary and secondary level for 30 years and continues treating children, adolescents, and their parents in private practice. Steve has worked closely with school community members to assess, design, and implement strength-based strategies in a school setting. Steve has presented at conferences for teachers, administrators, parents, and psychologists. For more information: www.drstevenbaron.com

Also Available from Routledge Eye On Education

www.routledge.com/k-12

**Student-Centered Literacy Assessment in the 6-12 Classroom:
An Asset-Based Approach**
Sean Ruday and Katie Caprino

**Teaching Resilience and Mental Health Across the
Curriculum: A Guide for High School and College Teachers**
Linda Yaron Weston

**Working Hard, Working Happy: Cultivating a Culture of
Effort and Joy in the Classroom**
Rita Platt

**The Student Motivation Handbook: 50 Ways to Boost an
Intrinsic Desire to Learn**
Larry Ferlazzo

Teaching with a Strength-Based Approach

How to Motivate Students and Build Relationships

Steven Baron

Routledge
Taylor & Francis Group

NEW YORK AND LONDON

Designed cover image: © Getty Images

First published 2023
by Routledge
605 Third Avenue, New York, NY 10158

and by Routledge
4 Park Square, Milton Park, Abingdon, Oxon, OX14 4RN

Routledge is an imprint of the Taylor & Francis Group, an informa business

ISBN: 9781032435831 (hbk)
ISBN: 9781032432571 (pbk)
ISBN: 9781003368014 (ebk)

DOI: 10.4324/9781003368014

Typeset in Palatino
by Newgen Publishing UK

Deep and abiding thanks to my wife, Tina, who never complained about my long hours working on the computer. You always supported my attempts to grow professionally and were totally on board with my dream of writing this book. To say I am grateful for your patience, support, and love is a vast understatement.

Matthew and Joshua thought the idea of their dad writing a book was cool. They both offered the much-needed encouragement that helped keep me going during the inevitable periods of frustration that arose during this project. Being your father inspires me to do the best I can for the children I treat.

May 2022

Contents

About the Author

Steven Baron served as a school psychologist at the elementary and secondary level for 30 years and continues treating children, adolescents, and their parents in private practice. Early in his career, he shifted from looking at what is wrong with the child to what is right, adopting a strength-based perspective emphasizing, identifying, and building on assets rather than focusing on eliminating deficits. Steve has worked closely with school community members to assess, design, and implement strength-based strategies in a school setting.

Steve's formal training includes obtaining certification as a school psychologist before completing a doctoral degree in school-community psychology, then obtaining postdoctoral training in child and adolescent psychotherapy. In addition to teaching at the college level, he has contributed articles on the strength-based model and facilitating communication in child therapy to various magazines and books. He authored a chapter on treating bullies in the book, *Play Therapy: A Comprehensive Guide to Theory and Practice* (Crenshaw and Stewart, eds) and a chapter on how school psychologists can use the strength-based model in *Play Therapy Interventions to Enhance Resilience* (Crenshaw, Brooks, and Goldstein, eds). He and David A. Crenshaw co-authored *Symbol Association Therapy Strategies-Child (SATS-C)*. Steve has presented at conferences for teachers, administrators, parents, and psychologists.

For more information: www.drstevenbaron.com

There is an ancient Chinese proverb that captures the essence of focusing on the strengths of a person beginning with what is inside of them and then expanding it to the world. It reads as follows:

> If there is light in the soul,
> there will be beauty in the person.
> If there is beauty in the person,
> there will be harmony in the house.
> If there is harmony in the house,
> there will be order in the nation.
> If there is order in the nation,
> there will be peace in the world.

Foreword

I have been a clinical psychologist and educator for 50 years. There have been several noteworthy changes that have transpired within the field of psychology since I first embarked on my professional journey. One of the most dramatic was a shift from a so-called "medical model" with its emphasis on "fixing deficits" in children and adults to a strength-based approach that directs us to identify and reinforce the strengths of individuals, strengths that I first referred to 40 years ago as "islands of competence." This shift is associated with the emergence of the field of "positive psychology" and a heightened interest in a concept that has been a cornerstone of my work: resilience.

My clinical practice has always included children, teens, and adults, prompting my focus on "resilience across the lifespan." Another shift in my perspective was to question, especially in my work with children and teens, the parameters of my role as a therapist and the context in which therapy takes place. For instance, initially I subscribed to the prevailing viewpoint that the practice of child therapy was confined of one's office with little, if any, contact with a child's parents or teachers. Typically, another clinician provided parent counseling, while communication with the child or adolescent's school rarely, if ever, occurred. Such an intervention model resulted in what I considered to be a fragmented, isolated approach that reduced the effectiveness of therapy.

I began to adopt a broader view of the role of a child and adolescent therapist, even during my training as a postdoctoral Fellow. The latter position included involvement with a therapeutic day program for students with behavioral and learning problems. As I spent time in the classrooms of this program, I witnessed skilled teachers who were able to touch both the minds and hearts of their students. Years later it led me to observe that some of the most effective therapists I have ever met did not call themselves therapists. Rather, they were classroom teachers. I asserted that in many ways they have a more profound impact on the lives of children than therapists might have; in saying this I was not minimizing my influence as a therapist but rather highlighting the lifelong influence of teachers.

This belief was further reinforced when I became principal of a school in a locked door unit in the child and adolescent program of a psychiatric hospital. It was during that time that I and my staff, feeling stressed and burned out ourselves, struggled with the seemingly Herculean task of providing a sound educational experience for angry and depressed children and teens with histories of school failure and a lack of trust in adults. We slowly recognized that our failed interventions were rooted in a constricted view of these students. We primarily perceived them as "out of control" youth, resulting in forms of discipline that were arbitrary and counterproductive. In focusing solely on their behaviors and diagnoses, we lost sight of their strengths and "islands of competence."

We came to appreciate that our students recognized our loss of faith in their capacity to improve, intensifying their lack of trust in us and their continued use of counterproductive behaviors. We knew that we had to change our approach if the students in our program were to begin to trust and learn from us. Often by trial and error we introduced what would now be labeled as "strength-based" strategies.

The seeds of my interest in hope and resilience were borne at this time. I remember searching for a resource that described specific, realistic strategies for not only working with our students in the psychiatric hospital but also for managing our own feelings of burnout as a staff of educators and clinicians.

Since that time greater attention has been paid to creating schools rooted in a strength-based model. A truly rich resource can now be found in Dr. Steve Baron's impressive book *Teaching with a Strength-Based Approach: How to Motivate Students and Build Relationships*. Having served as a school psychologist for many years and having consulted with many teachers about children in their classrooms, Steve possesses a wealth of experience in developing strength-based school programs for students that nurture their intrinsic motivation, caring, responsibility, self-discipline, and resilience.

I first met Steve about 12 years ago when he attended a couple of my seminars and a warm personal and professional friendship developed. His genuine caring for students and staff in his school and for clients in his private practice were quickly evident, as was the creativity he demonstrated in applying a strength-based perspective in all of his professional activities. I was so impressed with his interventions that I highlighted Steve's work in an article I posted on my website in 2012. The title reflected the nature of Steve's activities: "Searching for Strengths in the School Setting: To Enrich Dignity, Motivation, and Learning."

Since our initial meeting, Steve has continued to elaborate upon, lecture, and write about the strength-based concepts guiding his work. These concepts and strategies are now captured in this book. Steve shares in detail vignettes of interventions that have enriched the lives of students and that can be adopted by teachers and other school staff with all students in their schools. The power of Steve's strategies is that they are not only applicable to assist struggling students, but they can also be used within a preventative approach, namely, to create classroom environments that lessen the probability of learning and behavioral problems from emerging.

In light of the devastating effects of bullying on students, Steve includes a section on activities to minimize bullying from occurring within a strength-based classroom. In addition, he describes exercises that a teacher can use on the first day of school to begin the process of creating a supportive and welcoming classroom environment.

Steve's years as a school psychologist and his understanding of the daily challenges faced by teachers are skillfully addressed in this book. Just as Steve appreciates that students will learn and thrive in the presence of caring, empathic educators, he is aware that if the latter are to care for students, they must also learn to care for themselves. Citing the high incidence of stress and burnout among teachers and the growing numbers who leave the field within just a few years of entering the profession,

Steve provides realistic techniques for teachers to use to lessen their stress and disillusionment and to become what he calls "a strength-based teacher."

In reading Steve's book, I thought about how helpful his insights would have been as my staff and I struggled to create a strength-based school within a psychiatric hospital. These insights are now available in this book for educators to use in any school. Steve's wisdom, rooted in years of experience, takes on even greater urgency during these very challenging times not only in our schools but in all aspects of our society. His outlook of realistic optimism, coupled with realistic strategies, offers encouragement and hope.

I am certain Steve's book will be read and re-read not only by teachers, school staff, and professionals who consult with schools, but by parents as well. This book represents a rich resource for those of us who desire to create schools that support the wellbeing of staff and students alike.

Robert Brooks, Ph.D.
Faculty (part-time) Harvard Medical School
Co-author: *Raising Resilient Children; The Power of Resilience; Children's Classroom Behavior: Creating Sustainable, Resilient Classrooms*

Acknowledgments

While I am the author of this book, it was by no means a solitary pursuit. I have been incredibly blessed to have the encouragement, support, and practical assistance of a group of people I am indebted to in so many different ways. Without them, this book would not have happened at all.

I am grateful to count three giants in the strength-based world as colleagues and close friends. These three human beings practice what they preach and cultivate my passion for this model. I am grateful to have them in my life.

It was pure serendipity for me to take a summer workshop on child psychotherapy techniques – more years ago than I care to remember – with Dr. David Crenshaw. David's compassion for children in providing a corrective emotional experience in therapy is second to none. Besides being a wonderful mentor and teacher, his warmth, humor, and sensitivity are incredibly healing to the children whose lives he has touched. He is a pioneer in developing child therapy techniques to facilitate a therapeutic conversation with children, and I have incorporated many of his ideas in my clinical work. In addition, he is a social advocate providing a voice for those who are not heard. I am indebted to him for opening my eyes to the idea of becoming a writer when he asked me to co-author a book with him and, subsequently, contribute chapters to books he edited. I appreciate his advice along the way in writing this book. I am proud to count David as a close friend! It was through him that I met Dr. Robert Brooks.

Bob has written *the* book (in fact, many of them) on promoting resilience. His insights into providing a strength-based perspective in working with children have been inspirational for me. I read his monthly columns religiously. His ability to translate his ideas on strength-based practice into concrete and practical strategies for children, parents, and educators has served as a model for me and many others. In addition to being a source of practical advice for so many, Bob's knowledge of resilience and positive psychology makes him an incredibly respected leader in the field. His kindness, support, and willingness to make himself available to answer my questions were essential on a personal level. Bob was also indispensable in giving me a start as an author by inviting me to write a chapter for a book he edited. And although Bob is an ardent New England Patriots fan, while I am a lifelong New York Jets fan, we have never let football rivalry get in the way of our friendship, which I deeply cherish.

Charlie Appelstein is a strength-based therapist par excellence. His ability to connect with even the most troubled youth to allow them to see the repository of strengths inside of them is remarkable. I first met Charlie at a conference where he presented a strength-based model for traumatized children, which immediately resonated with me. He has always been remarkably generous in sharing ideas, many of which have profoundly influenced my clinical work. Professionally, I also owe Charlie a considerable debt of gratitude as he took a chance on using a new author to serve as the clinical editor of his book, *No Such Thing as a Bad Kid* (2nd ed.). I had never served in a position like that before, but Charlie requested that I share my feedback on what he wrote – and was always gracious in receiving it. This experience was crucial in helping mold my work in the strength-based model. In turn, I was fortunate to have Charlie serve as my clinical editor and sounding board during the writing of this book. His observations have gone a long way in helping me clarify my ideas. Charlie's wit, knowledge, and encouragement throughout the writing of this book helped keep me going when I had to deal with the unavoidable frustrations in writing. He is a valued friend.

Dr. Jonah Paquette is a psychologist who specializes in positive psychology and how emotions impact social/emotional functioning. I had the unique pleasure of first meeting Jonah at a weeklong workshop he taught on how positive psychology can enhance wellbeing. The clear, concise, and compelling manner in which he imparted the material to the class made it come alive and fostered my passion for this topic and desire to apply it in my clinical work. Jonah's several books on happiness, awe, and enhancing resilience have become go-to resources in formulating interventions. Jonah's commitment to the field of positive psychology is very palpable when he teaches, and he passes it on to his students.

My good friend, Melissa (Mel) Davis, who served as my writing editor, was invaluable during the book writing process. A lawyer, teacher, author, and fellow Beatles aficionado, Melissa was a stalwart in encouraging me to write this book and spread the value of mental health support for children. Her dedication to helping me present my ideas as clearly and concisely as possible is largely responsible for the book you are holding in your hands.

Dr. Howard Gurr provided heartfelt encouragement when it was most needed, allowing me to frankly discuss all the roadblocks in writing this book and helping me regain my focus when necessary.

Paula Litzky graciously shared her expertise in publishing, offering advice and a great deal of practical assistance. Her input was valuable in moving this book forward.

I also want to thank Portage & Main Press sincerely for allowing me to reproduce the graphic organizer, "Who Am I" Profile by Leyton Schnellert, Linda Watson, and Nicole Widdess. Deep appreciation also goes to Chris Wejr and Karen Copeland for allowing the inclusion of their "Exploring Our Own Strengths and Talents Template." Both of these are very useful tools allowing children to hone in on what they can do well. Finally deep thanks go to Margaret Rice, owner of YourTherapySource. com, for allowing me to share their very useful sentence completion exercise for teachers, entitled "Determine Student Strengths In The Classroom."

My unending gratitude goes to the staff of Routledge Publishing, who offered me the opportunity to share my passion for the strength-based model. In particular, I wish to acknowledge Lauren Davis, publisher at Routledge, for believing in the book's message and offering me the opportunity to publish it with such a renowned organization. In addition, many thanks go to Julia Giordano, Editorial Assistant at Routledge, for tolerating the many questions I threw at her and the outstanding practical assistance she provided.

My deep appreciation goes to the teachers I have been honored to share this work with over my years as a school psychologist. They are unsung heroes in our society. For 30 years, I had a front-row seat to observe how many of them rise above the obstacles they face to do all they can to touch their students' hearts, minds, and souls. I was truly inspired to witness this on a daily basis. I wrote this book for them, and if it can help them do their job in any way, then all the time and effort spent writing were well worth it.

Finally, a big thank you to all the children, adolescents, and families I have been privileged to have worked with and learned so much from during my years of practice. Parenting is the world's most challenging job, yet seeing the sacrifice and energy of parents validates my belief that most parents want what is best for their kids. I have come to respect all of you as you shared your vulnerabilities and concerns. This sacred trust, which I never took for granted, has made my journey as a psychologist incredibly enriching!

Introduction

Carl Jung, one of the founders of modern psychology, spoke eloquently about the crucial role teachers play in shaping the emotional development of their students.

> One looks back with appreciation to the brilliant teachers, but with gratitude to those who touched our human feelings. The curriculum is so much necessary raw material, but warmth is the vital element for the growing plant and for the soul of the child.[1]

Les Brown is a well-known motivational speaker on the topic of self-improvement. He was born in the Liberty City section of Miami on the floor of an abandoned building and experienced cruel hardship growing up.

Academically, Les had a great deal of difficulty in school. His school district classified him as "educable mentally handicapped" and retained him in the fifth grade. In contrast, he had a twin brother who was exceptionally bright and gifted, something Les's peers used to tease him about by calling him "DT" – the "dumb twin."

One day a teacher asked Les to solve a problem on the chalkboard, but Les refused and said that he could not do it. "Of course, you can," the teacher responded encouragingly. "Young man, come up here and solve this problem for me." Les was adamant. "I can't – I'm educable mentally handicapped." While the class

DOI: 10.4324/9781003368014-1

laughed, the teacher looked Les straight in the eye. "Don't ever say that again," the teacher told him firmly. "Someone else's opinion of you does not have to become your reality."[2] These words resonated with Les, who has indeed lived the phrase he became famous for: "You have greatness within you." Les became a broadcaster in later life and among his many accomplishments is his election to the Ohio House of Representatives.

The desire to write this book grew out of experiencing and witnessing the powerful impact of teachers' words. As a student and later as a school psychologist, I developed an appreciation of how impactful teachers are in the lives of their students. A pat on the shoulder, a kind word of encouragement, and perhaps a dose of tough love all go a long way toward expanding not only a student's understanding of the subject matter but of life itself. Of course, things can go the opposite way.

In tenth grade, I found myself having a great deal of difficulty in a geometry class. I genuinely felt lost in the class. After failing yet another math test, I was devastated. Getting up the nerve to approach the math teacher to tell him I did not understand anything about this subject took a great deal of effort. He asked what I did not understand, and when I answered, he looked at me and said, "Just forget about this, Steve. You will never figure it out. Maybe you should consider a career selling lady's underwear." And then … he laughed. I stood frozen and astounded! Was he serious? I had no idea how to react, said nothing, and walked to my seat, feeling defeated and deflated. I remember going home that day and telling my parents that continuing the math tutor they had hired to help me was "no use – I give up." Despite their attempts to boost my spirits, I felt as if the switch was already turned, and I resigned myself to failing math, which happened that semester and an additional one after that.

My tenth-grade math experience still produces anger, sadness, a sense of failure, and a strong desire to avoid anything to do with that subject. After years as a school psychologist, I have seen many instances of a student's hopes being either enhanced or deflated by the words or actions of a teacher. I have often seen children in counseling who are convinced their teachers were the personification of evil, become turned off, and then tuned out what was going on in the class. One child, in particular, told me, "I really hate her and will never do anything for that class." Unfortunately, nothing his parents or I could say changed his mindset about the teacher or the class.

As will be discussed in this book, the teacher-student relationship is the crucial variable in promoting student growth. While a thorough understanding of the academic subject matter is undoubtedly necessary, it is impossible to achieve that goal without the foundation of a sound teacher-student relationship. If that foundation is missing, any gains made occur in a sterile vacuum. The power of connection is the critical variable in helping our students learn, grow, and achieve.

When I begin psychotherapy with a new child, I always tell the parents that the indispensable element – apart from any skill or talent I offer – will be the relationship forged between their child and me. Having a child feel safe, secure, understood, and respected is the bedrock of any successful therapeutic intervention. Psychotherapy outcome research identifies the therapeutic alliance as the primary factor for patient growth in therapy.[3]

Given the importance of the therapeutic alliance, it is a natural extension to consider the variable of the teacher-student relationship in reviewing the conditions necessary for success in school. However, in this age of accountability, teachers have to gear their lessons toward standardized tests, which may, in turn, be tied to evaluating the overall competence of the teacher. I am concerned that this connection is getting short-changed. While we may be teaching students valuable content, the experience does not necessarily enhance a child's inner growth. Instead, in the understandable haste to make sure the material is covered, teachers may focus on the finish line rather than helping their students take the time to absorb and truly understand the information – and enjoy the journey in getting there.

Thirty years of experience as a school psychologist provided me with innumerable opportunities to examine the crucial role of teacher-student connections in promoting success – or failure. I felt motivated to write this book to extoll the virtues of that all-important connection and provide teachers with a model to facilitate positive student-teacher relationships. I have also included specific methods and exercises to help create that connection. Utilizing the ideas put forth in this book will improve a student's chances for success. Consider this a manual on using your relationship with your students to put them in the best possible position to succeed while becoming happier and more fulfilled.

One of the essential points of this book is that there cannot be a separation between promoting a solid relationship with students and teaching the curriculum – they go hand in hand. Teacher and student satisfaction with their roles can – and should – be invigorated and enhanced.

In my work with teachers, students, and parents, I use a strength-based model. This perspective values strengths and assets and aims to develop them rather than spend time and resources repairing deficits. As discussed in Chapter 3, this model can be a potent tool teachers can use to form connections with students, encourage the development of their self-esteem, and position them for success. The focus of the teacher-student relationship, combined with a strength-based perspective, offers hope, encouragement, and greater confidence for students, teachers, and parents.

I hope to communicate that the relationship you have with your students is a powerful way to appeal to the desire of all children to be competent, self-assured, and resilient. A trusted relationship is vital to any learning process throughout life, whether with a parent, coach, or teacher. When students feel they are in a secure, trusted relationship, insecurities, fears, and doubts will begin to break down and eventually collapse. Having such a relationship with a teacher will enable a student to feel inspired and achieve. Focusing on these social-emotional processes will not short-circuit the learning process but greatly enhance it. Students will be likely to internalize the goals and values of their teachers and become more motivated to succeed when they feel they are genuinely cared for by their teachers.

This is not speculation based on anecdotal reports. Scientific evidence conclusively proves that the teacher-student relationship is a critical ingredient in student success and adaptation. Students need to believe that they can make positive changes in their lives. One way students can genuinely internalize this belief is via the interactions they engage in with others. As Nan

Henderson, a leader in resiliency building in education, notes, "The most critical resiliency builder for every student is a basic trusting relationship, even with just one adult, within the family or without, that says, 'you matter.'"[4]

The Commission on Children at Risk, a panel of physicians, research scientists, and youth service professionals, has stated, "the basic conclusion of this report is that children are hardwired for close connections with others and for moral and spiritual meaning."[5] The role of connection in school is quite simply the basis for student success.

Jim Cummins, a professor at the Ontario Institute for Studies in Education of the University of Toronto, notes:

> Human relationships are the heart of schooling. The interactions between students and teachers and among students are more central to student success than any method of teaching literacy, or science, or math. When strong relationships are established between teachers and students, these relationships frequently can transcend the economic and social disadvantages that afflict communities and schools alike.[6]

Never underestimate your potential to influence a student. Little do you know the impact you can have on a child that can resonate long after they are in your classroom.

When I was contemplating a career as a psychologist, others would ask why I chose this field. My answer was always, "I want to make a difference in the lives of others and help them be the best version of themselves." Over 30 years later, that sentiment continues to ring true for me.

Despite numerous obstacles, most teachers still want to create an atmosphere where their students can acquire academic knowledge and become more confident and self-assured. This notion of "making a difference" in the lives of children is often listed as one of the primary reasons people go into teaching.[7] This book aims to help you tap into that motivation and see it practically applied in your work with students. My fervent hope is that reading this book will stimulate or reawaken your desire to connect with a student's psyche in the most meaningful way possible.

References

1. Patterson, K. (2010). *Teaching In Troubled Times*. Pembroke Publishers.
2. www.wabisabilearning.com/blog/4-stories-great-teachers
3. Diener, M., Hilsenroth, M., & Weinberger, J. (2007). "Therapist affect focus and patient outcomes in psychodynamic psychotherapy: A meta-analysis." *The American Journal of Psychiatry*, 164(6), 936–41. https://search.proquest.com/docview/220470637?accountid= 35022.

   See also Weissmark, M. & Giacomo, D. (1995). "Measuring therapeutic interactions: Research and clinical applications." *Psychiatry*, 58(2), 173–88. https://search.proquest.com/docview/220700 806?accountid=35022

   See also Beauford, J., McNiel, D., & Binder, R. (1997). "Utility of the initial therapeutic alliance in evaluating psychiatric patients' risk of violence." *The American Journal of Psychiatry*, 154(9), 1272–6. https:// search.proquest.com/docview/220477523?accountid=35022

   See also Whiston, S. (1996). "Accountability through action research: Research methods for practitioners." *Journal of Counseling and Development*, 74(6), 616. doi: http://dx.doi.org/10.1002/j.1556-6676.1996.tb02301.x;\

   See also Bedi, R. (2004). "The therapeutic alliance and the interface of career counseling and personal counseling." *Journal of Employment Counseling*, 41(3), 126–35. doi: http://dx.doi.org/ 10.1002/j.2161-1920.2004.tb00886.x
4. Henderson, N. & Milstein, M. (2003). *Resiliency In Schools*. Corwin Press.
5. Henderson, N. (2007). *Resiliency In Action*, 2nd ed. Resiliency in Action.
6. Alberta Mentoring Partnership. (2022, January, 26). "Creating Strength-Based Classroom and Schools." https://wrap2fasd.org/ 2022/01/26/creating-strength-based-classroom-and-schools/
7. Teacher Tapp. (2019, July, 10). 4 Reasons People become Teachers. https://teachertapp.co.uk/4-reasons-people-become-teachers/

1

What Unique Problems Do Teachers Face?

So often, comedians have a way of stating the truth even though it is in an amusing way. Seth Meyers, the well-known comedian, was able to do that by stripping down to the essence of what it means to be a teacher in a funny but accurate quote.

> Don't F*** with Teachers. They make no money, and they get up at 6 A.M to drive their 15-year-old cars to a cruddy building knee-deep in teenage hormones. You can't scare them. The part of them that is capable of fear was burned away years ago by terrible teacher's lounge coffee, and all they want is health care, a livable wage, and just once a class that doesn't laugh the first time, they hear the word "Uranus."[1]

In front of you sit 15, 20, 25, or more students, their eyes trained on you. These students – as well as their parents and school administrators – are looking to you to enlighten, educate, and encourage them to grow and reach their fullest potential. Society, too, is watching – and depending on your success. The responsibility of being a teacher, coach, and therapist is daunting, but it may be part of why you became a teacher in the first place. You could be feeling scared, nervous, exhilarated, and inspired – all at the same

DOI: 10.4324/9781003368014-2

time. The prospect of handing down knowledge and teaching skills while helping a child or adolescent reach their potential is what a teacher strives for every day of their career. You are ready to get to work and make a real difference in the lives of your students.

The challenge is there, and you are ready to take it on! However, as you will learn – or maybe have already learned – standing in front of a class, engaging with students is not the only part of your job. Far from it. You are expected to wear many hats. Besides conveying information, and monitoring student behavior within the classroom, in the halls, and other common areas, you are also in charge of directing student interaction. You are also expected to communicate with parents, confer with colleagues, and interface with administrators. Within these responsibilities lie many additional tasks you may never have imagined being responsible for when you were in college or graduate school preparing to become a teacher.

In addition to managing all these obligations, which can significantly decrease the time you have available for students, forces outside your control are at work that can also erode your motivation and desire to be creative and engaging in the classroom. The good intentions you had when you decided to become a teacher can wither, and what was once a hugely exciting endeavor can become a highly pressured, energy-sapping struggle. Despite your original intent to give your best to your students, achieving that noble goal can become harder than you ever imagined.

These factors, plus others discussed within this book, are not of your creation, but unfortunately, many of them come with the territory. Blaming yourself in this scenario is unfair and will only serve to wear down your drive to be the best teacher you can be. Consider the following obstacles that continually rear their heads – and have nothing to do with you.

Lack of Control Over What You Do

Much research confirms that feeling little control over what we do will lead to disengagement from the task, and our physical and mental health will pay the price. One study found that in a sample of over 7,000 employees, those who experienced little or no control over the deadlines imposed on them had a significantly higher rate of coronary disease.[2] In another study, nursing home residents who had control over simple tasks, such as caring for plants, reported greater levels of life satisfaction and a longer lifespan.[3]

What do disgruntled office workers and contented senior citizens have in common with teachers? It turns out quite a lot. In the 21st century, many school districts have seen their curriculum revamped by new state and federal guidelines. Instead of having the chance to use your creativity to improvise in your classroom to meet your students' unique needs, you are now required to follow increasingly rigid rules. Teachers have reported feeling frustrated by not being able to deviate from a curriculum strictly prescribed from outside the classroom and frequently from outside the school or district. There is minimal opportunity to include strategies and methods that may be fruitful as they do not fully coincide with what is expected or allowed by state education departments. I recall a Language Arts teacher telling me that she could no longer infuse her lessons with writing strategies she had successfully used many times over the years to enhance the creative writing abilities of her students. She was now forbidden from using them as they were seen as detrimental to the goals of the new curriculum; instead, she was forced to follow the rules set out by the school or district administration, often imposed by the state or federal government. Having more significant input in what you do goes a long way to enhance the motivation and commitment of both students and teachers.

Instruction is now geared toward preparing students to do well on standardized tests. The opportunity for teachers to introduce concepts and material that may not be germane to these tests is minimal, and doing so is strongly discouraged. Further, there is little time for teachers to respond to questions raised by students. Many teachers no longer have the "luxury" of reviewing areas where students need more practice to become adept with the material to be tested, respond to students' questions, or foster genuine curiosity in topics that have piqued their interest.

Budget Concerns

Teachers are asked to do more with less. Strikes have occurred in several locales within the United States, with teachers protesting wages, increased class size, and fewer resources. Mandates fall on districts to fund increasing administrative costs and programs that eat up a large percentage of a district's budget. Determining annual school budgets has become a political football in some communities with a reluctant tax base. The increasing cost of school supplies is just one factor that has significantly cut into resources. In many districts, teachers "foot" the bill out of their own pocket for school supplies for students or the classroom. With less money for resources, teacher salaries are also impacted. It is not uncommon for teachers to take on additional jobs to help make ends meet. Approximately 20 percent of teachers work during the summer and have a second job at nights and weekends during the school year.[4] That means there is less time available for teachers to work on curriculum, write lesson plans, catch up on professional reading, or attend workshops to develop their skills. Many teachers need to supplement their income because, on average, teachers nationally earned 78.6 cents on the dollar in 2018 compared to the earnings of other college graduates – and much less than the inflation-adjusted 93.7 cents on the dollar teachers earned more than 20 years earlier in 1996.[5]

Increasing Administrative Responsibilities

The days when teachers were only responsible for drafting lesson plans and focusing primarily on standing in front of their class to present those plans are long gone. As many teachers will tell you, actual teaching time is only a fraction of what they are required to do.

In one survey, public school teachers were asked to break down their job responsibilities.[6] The results were as follows:

Classroom Preparation – 30%
Teaching in the Classroom – 25%

Grading Student Work – 20%
Administration – 15%
Personal Attention to Students – 4%
Coaching – 3%
Parent Interaction – 3%

Not only is the amount of classroom instructional time less than that spent grading student work and completing administrative tasks combined, but the amount of attention given to students on an individual basis is only slightly more than the time devoted to parent interaction. Five times more attention is given to grading student work than to actually giving the student personal attention and almost as much as presenting the material initially.

Increased Competition for Student Attention

Teachers have discovered that they have to stand out in the crowd for students to notice them, pay attention to what they are saying, and buy into what is happening in class. Growing up in the 1960s and 1970s in New York City, long before the advent of cable television, I had access to only seven television channels. In contrast, hundreds of television channels offer a massive array of content in contemporary society. However, these are only a tiny number of available options for children (and adults) to distract and entertain themselves. You do not even need to be in front of a television; modern technology has made it unbelievably easy to access content across various platforms. This has crept into schools, with schools forced to regulate student use of cell phones during class time.

In a recent study, the American Hospital Association reported that, on average, children and teenagers ages 8–18 spend more than seven hours per day looking at screens.[7] This is time that could otherwise be available for academic activities like homework or extra-credit work, or after-school activities such as music lessons, sports, scouting, or working at a job such as babysitting or lawn mowing.

A prevalent complaint I hear from parents is that while computers are required for school assignments, they also provide unlimited distractions for their children. Despite software limiting what students can view, it is remarkable how easily children can find ways to access content that interests them while doing their homework, even – and perhaps especially – content they should not necessarily be viewing. Parents and teachers discovered how "tech-savvy" students could be during the COVID pandemic when students had to depend on remote learning.

School Violence

Regrettably, once simply unimaginable, this has become a modern-day fact of life for students, teachers, administrators, and parents as we are all too often reminded by eerily familiar scenes playing out on television. School shootings are becoming a more frequent occurrence. However, bullying, intimidation, and sexual harassment, which have always been facets of the school experience, continue to impact a student's learning capacity. In fact, in 2018, 82 school shootings occurred in the United States, the highest number ever recorded.[8] In 2015, 3 percent of students in the United States reported a fear of being attacked or harmed in school.[9]

Teachers need to be attuned to their student's emotional state and act swiftly to secure assistance from the administration. As this book was being written, a tragic incident in Oxford, Michigan occurred with students and teachers killed and injured. An alert teacher spotted the drawings and writings of a disturbed student and brought them to the attention of the school administration. These situations require teachers to better understand their students' emotional well-being and discern when students are at risk and require immediate intervention.

It is also noteworthy to consider that the techniques used to keep schools safe may raise student anxiety. Data suggest that school lockdown drills can significantly affect children's mental health, increasing a student's fear of possible danger. While students report feeling more prepared after a lockdown drill, they also feel more vulnerable to an actual attack happening in their school. Depending on their age and cognitive functioning, many students may not fully discern between an actual incident and a drill. A recent study based on social media posts found that active shooter drills in schools correlated with a 42 percent increase in anxiety and stress and a 39 percent increase in depression among the entire school community, including students, teachers, and parents.[10]

Poverty

The impact of poverty on students cannot be overlooked or overestimated. Approximately one in seven (14.4 percent) American children lived in poverty in 2019, the most recent year for which statistics are available.[11] In 2019, 3.6 million children under the age of six lived in poverty, with just over 15 percent being infants, toddlers, and preschoolers. In breaking the numbers down further, 20.5 percent of children of color were considered poor in the United States, 2.5 times more likely to be poor than their white, non-Hispanic peers.

The impact of poverty on a child includes more than poorer health and a potentially shorter life span than their peers. These children lag behind those not living in poverty in growth, academic readiness, and school attendance. They are more likely to drop out of high school and less likely to pursue post-secondary education. In addition, the emotional health of these students is at risk, with higher rates of behavioral difficulties, such as truancy, bullying, and substance abuse.[12]

Increased Rates of Childhood Psychopathology

The incidence of mental illness in children and adolescents has exponentially increased over the past 20 years. The most recent statistics are revealing.[13] While the incidence of mental illness has been reported as increasing, authorities debate whether this may be due to an actual higher incidence or improved diagnostic tools.

- ◆ More than 7 percent of children aged 3–17 years (approximately 4.5 million) have been diagnosed with a behavior problem.
- ◆ ADHD, behavior problems, anxiety, and depression are the most commonly diagnosed mental disorders in children.
- ◆ Over 9 percent of children aged 2–17 years (approximately 6.1 million) have received an ADHD diagnosis.
- ◆ Seven percent of children aged 3–17 years (approximately 4.4 million) have been diagnosed with anxiety.
- ◆ Thirteen percent of boys aged 3–17 years and 36 percent of girls (approximately 1.9 million) have been diagnosed with depression. In fact, by the time adolescents turn 17, 13.6 percent of boys and a staggering 36.15 percent of girls have been or are depressed. These numbers are significantly higher than previous estimates.
- ◆ Data from the United States Substance Abuse and Mental Health Services Administration confirm that major depressive episodes among adolescents aged 12–17 increased by over 50 percent from 2005 to 2015. More adolescents in the United States in the late 2010s experienced severe psychological distress, suicidal thoughts, attempted suicide, and took their own lives than ever before.[14]
- ◆ Over seven million children in the United States are prescribed psychotropic medication annually.[15]
- ◆ Five percent of the children in the United States have IEPs (Individualized Educational Plans) and are classified as emotionally disabled, while 9 percent are classified as autistic.[16]

These considerations have dramatically altered the composition of mainstream classrooms; teachers are required to serve as armchair mental health counselors and deal with behavioral issues stemming from these issues. This affects how teachers provide content to their students, allocate their instruction time, and utilize their classroom management skills. While the number of students with identifiable mental health conditions is high, it is fair to say that many students are not formally diagnosed despite presenting significant emotional challenges. The reality is that school districts cannot afford to hire as many mental health counselors as may be needed to serve the student population, so teachers are increasingly called upon to meet this need whether they are ready – or not!

In addition, an increasing number of students have been the victim of trauma, exposure to a highly stressful event that overwhelms their ability to cope. This can include being a victim of or witness to physical or sexual abuse. Among the psychological impacts of such violence are feelings of helplessness, a lessened sense of self, and significant difficulty in being able to experience a range of emotions. Various psychological conditions, including PTSD (post-traumatic stress disorder), can be diagnosed in children as young as preschool age. Unfortunately, it is difficult to obtain statistics regarding the frequency of traumatic events in childhood as the criteria used to diagnose children may not be sufficiently developed. Nonetheless, if possible, teachers need to be aware of traumatic events in a child's life that impact their classroom functioning.

How Teachers' Perceptions of Their Profession Affect Their Performance

The Global Teacher Status Index is a survey that measures teachers' attitudes on various subjects. Relevant to the present discussion, teachers rated their profession lower than the public rated it. In one study of teachers in the United States, just 34 percent felt valued by society compared to 68 percent in Singapore.[17] In this sample 47 percent of teachers leave the profession within the first five years, while the average has been 17 percent nationally. From 1998 to 2018, the teacher attrition rate in Georgia nearly doubled, with 16–30 percent of teachers leaving the field annually.[18] Interestingly, 66 percent of teachers reported they were unlikely/very unlikely to recommend teaching to their high school students as a career choice in Georgia. As one teacher responded, "The profession has become less and less encouraging; it expects *a lot* [emphasis added] in return and maintains a punitive culture that essentially strikes fear, anxiety, and burnout."[19]

These factors combine to heavily influence the dynamics of the teacher-student relationship for better or worse. How can teachers and students, administrators, and parents rise above these conditions to form a team that fosters resiliency, and social and emotional growth, let alone meet academic benchmarks for students?

That is the question this book will address using the strength-based teaching model as a framework for teachers to reach out to their students and promote and build effective teacher-student relationships.

References

1. Seth Meyers. (2018, March 6). Late Night with Seth Meyers (Television Show) NBC www.pinterest.es/pin/33150722257 1610951/

2. Syme, L. & Balfour, J. (1997). "Explaining inequalities in coronary heart disease." *The Lancet*, 350, pp. 231–232.

3. Rodin, J. & Langer, E. (1977). "Long-term effects of a control-relevant intervention with the institutionalized aged." *Journal of Personality and Social Psychology*, 35(12), pp. 897–902.

4. Schaeffer, K. (2019, July 1). "About one-in-six U.S. teachers work second jobs – and not just in the summer." Pew Research Center. www.pewresearch.org/fact-tank/2019/07/01/about-one-in-six-u-s-teachers-work-second-jobs-and-not-just-in-the-summer/\

5. Freedberg, L. (2019, May 1). "Wage gap between teachers and other college graduates exacerbates teacher shortages." https://edsource.org/2019/wage-gap-between-teachers-and-other-college-graduates-exacerbates-teacher-shortages/611 728#:~:text=On%20average%2C%20teachers%20nationally%20 earned,over%20the%20past%20two%20decades

6. Hardison, H. (2022, April 19). "How teachers spend their time: A breakdown." *Education Week*. www.edweek.org/teaching-learning/how-teachers-spend-their-time-a-breakdown/2022/04

7. Welch, A. (2018, August 6). "Health experts say parents need to drastically cut kids' screen time." CBS News. www.cbsnews.com/news/parents-need-to-drastically-cut-kids-screen-time-devices-american-heart-association/

8. Campus Safety. (2018, October 15). "51 years of data: K-12 school shooting statistics everyone should know." *Campus Safety Magazine* www.campussafetymagazine.com/safety/K-12-school-shooting-statistics-everyone-should-know/

9. U.S. Department of Education, National Center for Education Statistics. (2018). Indicators Of School Crime and Safety: 2017. https://nces.ed.gov/fastfacts/display.asp?id=49

10. Kingkade, T. (2020, September 3). "Active shooter drills are meant to prepare students. But research finds 'severe' side effects." www.nbcnews.com/news/us-news/active-shooter-drills-are-meant-prepare-students-research-finds-severe-n1239103

11. Children's Defense Fund. (2022). The State of America's Children: Child Poverty 2021. www.childrensdefense.org/state-of-americas-children/soac-2021-child-poverty/

12. Murphy, D. & Redd, Z. (2014, January 18). "Five ways poverty harms children." www.childtrends.org/publications/5-ways-poverty-harms-children

13. Center For Disease Control and Prevention. (2022, June 3). Data and Statistics on Children's Mental Health. www.cdc.gov/childrensmentalhealth/data.html

14. Twenge, J., Joiner, T., Duffy, M., Cooper A., & Binau, S. (2019). "Age, period, and cohort trends in mood disorders indicators and suicide-related outcomes in a nationally representative dataset, 2005–2017." *Journal of Abnormal Psychology*, 126(3), 185–199.

15. Citizen's Commission on Human Rights International. (2022). Number of Children and Adolescents Taking Psychiatric Drugs in the U.S. www.cchrint.org/psychiatric-drugs/children-on-psychiatric-drugs/

16. National Center of Education Statistics. (2018, May). The Condition of Education 2018. https://nces.ed.gov/pubs2018/2018144.pdf

17. Dolton, P. & Marcenaro-Gutierrez, O. (2013). Global Teacher Status Index. (2013, October) www.globalteacherprize.org/media/2787/2013globalteacherstatusindex.pdf

18. Owens, S. (2015, December) Georgia's Teacher Dropout Crisis. Georgia Department of Education. www.gadoe.org/External-Affairs-and-Policy/communications/Documents/Teacher%20Survey%20Results.pdf
19. Ascione, L. (2018, February, 23). "7 days of twitter chats." *E School News*. www.eschoolnews.com/2018/02/page/2/

2

What Is the Impact of Teacher-Student Relationships on School Life?

Jim Henson, the beloved creator of the Muppets, summed up what he believes kids remember about their teachers, saying,

Kids don't remember what you try to teach them.
They remember what you are.[1]

***

It was in first grade that I initially encountered my problems with reading. I didn't learn to read as quickly as other kids. Back then, if you were slow to read, your diagnosis was obvious: Stupid.

In some schools, those in charge used shame and humiliation to motivate slow readers – standing in the corner or wearing a dunce cap. In some schools, kids would get spanked.

I was lucky. I had a first-grade teacher … Mrs. Eldredge who knew that there was more to little boys and girls who were slow readers than being stupid, and there were better ways to help them than by shaming or punishing them. She'd been teaching first grade for a long time.

DOI: 10.4324/9781003368014-3

Mrs. Eldredge was … very kind, but she could also be tough, so no one messed with her. During the reading period … when my turn would come, Mrs. Eldredge would take a seat beside me and put her arm around me. Her arm took away any embarrassment I might have felt as I stammered and stumbled over the words. None of the other kids laughed at me because I had the enforcer sitting next to me.

Her kind nature and soft arm took out the damaging disabilities: fear, shame, and believing something was wrong with me. Mrs. Eldredge's arm is what we would call now my IEP, my individualized educational plan and it was the best IEP ever devised.

Had I had a different first-grade teacher, I likely would have acquired the toxic disabilities of shame, fear, and selling myself short. I will always be grateful to Mrs. Eldredge for giving me such an excellent start.[2]

This wonderful vignette is from Dr. Edward Hallowell. Subsequently diagnosed as having ADHD, he is now an esteemed psychiatrist and one of the world's leading authorities on that disorder. Dr. Hallowell's story eloquently captures how powerful and life-changing a child's relationship with a caring, supportive teacher can be. Mrs. Eldredge intuitively knew the relationship she forged with the little boy who would grow up to be Dr. Hallowell could potentially transform his life – and it did.

The importance of connecting with our students cannot be overstated. This variable transcends imparting facts or being able to have students recall dates. Instead, it is an intangible that permeates how effective we will be in reaching our goals as teachers and how our students will fare during the rest of their school days – and beyond.

This is not a new notion. The impact of the teacher-student relationship on student academic and social growth has been studied for over 50 years. Some of this early research will be cited, along with more current findings, to provide a solid con-text for understanding how crucial is our connection to students.

Teaching is not just about applying rote techniques, and learning does not occur in a vacuum; students respond to their teacher's attitudes, as well as their verbal and nonverbal communications. Long after students learn math and spelling, their self-perception will figure in their everyday life – in their work, their relationships, and their ability to build successful lives; that self-perception will have been significantly shaped by their interactions with their teachers. Having a caring relationship with at least one person in a school setting significantly reduces school misconduct and violence rates, as recently supported by the United States Department of Education.

> Research shows that a positive relationship with an adult who is available to provide support when needed is one of the most critical factors in preventing student violence. Students often look to adults in the school community for guidance, support, and direction. Some children need help overcoming feelings of isolation and need support in developing connections to others. Effective schools make sure that opportunities exist for adults to spend quality, personal time with children.[3]

Making the time to connect with students for at least a few minutes on a daily basis is clearly time well spent.

Children who experienced abuse, trauma, or suffer from significant mental illness yet survive or even flourish in later life have one variable in common: the presence of an adult whom the child felt cared about them and offered unwavering support. It has been established that students in schools with a culture of fostering caring relationships between teachers and students are less likely to exhibit emotional dysfunction, substance abuse, and aggressive behavior.[4]

Students who feel safe, secure, and understood in the classroom will feel empowered to perform at higher academic and social levels than students who lack these feelings. Positive bonds with teachers make classrooms secure bases from which students can spread their wings and take academic and social risks. This cuts across all socioeconomic levels. Students in low-income groups with strong teacher-student relationships have higher academic achievement and more positive social-emotional functioning than their peers who lack such a relationship.[5]

Psychologist Jules Segal labels an adult who provides such a relationship to a child a "charismatic adult." This is not a person who has a lively personality, but rather "a person with whom children identify and from whom they can gather strength."[6] In many cases, that person is a teacher. Segal writes, "Small wonder that teachers often provide the magical bond that allows many children to turn their lives from certain defeat to glorious victory."[7]

For so many students, your classroom is their last stronghold. I recall a 15-year-old student who resided in a mental health facility. Before entering her current school, the student had behavioral difficulties. However, after the change in placement, the problematic behaviors disappeared, and she performed at a very high level both academically and behaviorally. When asked about this change, the student replied that she "loved going to school," adding, "I wish it were open seven days a week. I feel lost without being here." This student felt connected, understood, and safe, which is the foundation for any learning to occur.

How can you become a charismatic adult for your students? Segal proposes three ways to get that process going.[8]

First, as the old song goes: "Accentuate the positive."[9] Make a genuine attempt to focus on those things a student can do well and zero in on their strengths rather than their shortcomings. Concentrating on student assets rather than identifying their deficits reinforces their capabilities. According to the adage, "You can catch more flies with honey than vinegar."

Second, always emphasize the effort rather than the outcome of a student's attempts, even if they fail. If students come to believe their efforts are futile, they quite simply will give up. Instill an attitude in your students that defeats are merely temporary bumps in the road to success.

Third, understand that children, just like adults, are wired differently from each other. Children vary significantly on behavioral dimensions such as activity level, introversion and extraversion, adaptability to novel situations, and modulating their expression of emotion and self-control. Help your students understand that their individuality is something you appreciate.

Segal's observations set the stage for developing the strength-based philosophy in the classroom. Being a strength-based educator directs a teacher's interactions with students from Day One. The relationship will start growing organically as you interact with them to promote hope, confidence, and resilience. Communicating to your students how excited you are to be their teacher and how much you value them will foster an alliance. The closer the connection, the easier it will be for students to accept the messages you want to convey. Being positive and strength-based will promote strong relationships with students.

A positive, strength-based approach starts from the moment you meet your students and is all about conveying an attitude that says "I believe in you. I am thrilled to be your teacher. I know you will be successful with me." Everything you do from that moment on will extend this inspirational attitude. This is what builds great relationships!

I have met teachers who stand by the door to their room every morning or before every class and look each student in the eye as they enter, smile, and say "good morning," in addition to adding a statement such as "I'm glad you here" or "we are going to have fun today!" Sometimes they would compliment the student on their clothes or appearance. Doing this, especially at the start of the school year as you are both getting to know each other, is critical in building a valued connection. Finding out your students' interests outside of school and talking informally about these will help students feel comfortable and happy to be around you. I also recall a teacher who had several Mets baseball fans in her class. In addition to spending a few minutes talking about the previous day's game, she would also wear team jerseys to class and give less homework on the day after the team won. Because of her enthusiastic attitude, her students looked forward to coming to class and were eager to discuss the previous day's game.

This example demonstrates how being a strength-based teacher does not mean that you apply strategies in a rigidly prescribed manner. Instead, it is an attitude you convey to your students. Your attitudes are potent mediums that influence how your students respond to you – sometimes in very subtle ways. Students can be remarkably adept at tuning into the beliefs of others.

An early study of how teachers' attitudes impact student success was conducted in the 1960s by social psychologist Robert Rosenthal.[10] At the beginning of the school year, he informed teachers that particular students in their class had been evaluated and found to have high cognitive potential. The progress of the students was followed for the school year. Those students who had been identified as very intelligent experienced greater success academically compared to their non-identified peers. This high level of success was consistent for the entire year. In addition, these students did not demonstrate significant social-emotional or behavioral difficulties.

Rosenthal discovered that the teachers' expectations influenced their interactions with these particular students. For instance, these students had been given more time to answer questions and provided more specific feedback. On a nonverbal level, these teachers smiled, nodded, and appropriately touched these students with a pat on the shoulder more frequently. At the end of the school year, Rosenthal revealed that the identified students had never been formally assessed, but had been randomly selected. *Despite this, the identified group outperformed the rest of the class!*

Rosenthal's methods were criticized as the teachers in the study were deliberately misled; however, the results are still intriguing. Qualitative and quantitative differences in how the students in the selected group performed compared to the non-identified students were observed. The teachers in the study provided these particular students with enhanced support based on their beliefs about them – and the students responded. The mindset of the teachers was identified as an essential variable impacting how these students performed.

In one retrospective study, students were asked to rate their teachers' positive and negative traits.[11] Not surprisingly, teachers' positive traits influenced student attitudes toward school to a greater degree than negative ones. Additional research indicates that teachers' perceptions impact student success in academic subjects and behavior from elementary school through college.[12] When students experience teachers as caring, they put forth significantly more effort in the classroom. This finding has been replicated for diverse learners across cultures and countries.[13,14]

Many studies found that strong teacher-student relationships were tied to improvements on various crucial measures, including higher student engagement with academic content, improved attendance, a decline in disruptive behaviors and suspensions, and lower dropout rates. In addition, students who had positive relationships with teachers were less likely to engage in bullying behavior.[15] This connection was still quite strong even after controlling for differences in students' individual, family, and school backgrounds.[16] Related to this is the finding that middle and high school students who perceive their relationships with their teachers as supportive and warm are motivated to become more engaged in school and improve their academic performance.[17]

The impact of how their teachers relate to them can be felt by students as young as preschool age. In one study, preschoolers were divided into two groups in which they received lessons on socialization with peers. While both groups learned the same content, the way the teachers related to the students differed. In one group, the teachers had been instructed to be amiable and nurturing, for the purposes of the study only, while in the second group, they were told to act in a detached and remote manner. The students in the group led by teachers acting warmly were much more helpful to peers following the lesson than those who worked with the teachers acting in a detached way. The study concluded that *how* the teachers related to the students was more important than *what* they said.[18]

Student expectations of their classroom experience are shaped primarily by their perceptions of teacher expectations. Students who perceived that their teachers had high expectations of their academic achievement were more motivated to meet those expectations than peers who perceived low teacher expectations. For instance, less positive relationships with math teachers in middle school were associated with a decline in math performance in subsequent years. In contrast, more positive relationships were associated with improved levels of math performance.[19]

High school students with positive relationships with their teachers experience more positive academic and social outcomes.[20,21] When high school students feel their teachers care for them and are invested in their success, they report a greater desire to stay in school and explore future goals, such as higher education, more fully.[22] These relationships also impact the ability of students to master transition periods, such as from elementary to middle school and middle school to high school.[23]

Further, the quality of student interaction with teachers can affect their classmates' perceptions of them. If students view a peer as having primarily negative interactions with teachers (or conversely, if they identify a student as a "teacher's pet"), that will negatively impact their desire to seek out and interact with their classmate.[24]

Good teacher-student relationships benefit shy children who face isolation, loneliness, and depression. In one study, over 1200 students from third through seventh grade provided self-reports and teacher ratings to measure their levels of depression, loneliness, perceived popularity, and relationships with peers. While shy students were not rated highly on peers' popularity ratings, shy children who had a better relationship with their teachers often had fewer interpersonal difficulties in school. Other research suggests improved student grades are evident when they report positive relationships with teachers.[25]

In another study, students and teachers filled out questionnaires assessing their views on various school concerns. Students who strongly agreed that they had at least one teacher who made them "feel excited about the future" or that their school was "committed to building each student's strengths" were significantly more likely to demonstrate greater engagement with teachers than students who disagreed with those statements.[26]

Positive teacher-student relationships can also benefit a student's long-term health. Over 20,000 students were followed in a longitudinal study for 13 years, beginning in seventh grade when they were 12 to 13 years old. Students who reported better relationships with middle school and high school teachers also had better physical and mental health levels in their mid-20s.[27] This relationship also works inversely. Researchers in Canada tracked stress hormones in over 400 elementary school students. They found that teachers who reported higher levels of burnout had students with higher levels of the stress hormone cortisol each morning. Perhaps classroom tensions may be contagious?[28]

In another study, novice teachers were interviewed over the school year. Not surprisingly, those who reported higher stress levels at the start of the year were judged by their superiors as ineffective in providing explicit instruction, maintaining effective classroom management, and creating a stimulating classroom environment than teachers with lower initial stress levels.[29] Another study found that a teacher's relationship with students was the best predictor of the level of happiness or anxiety experienced by the teacher.[30]

As empirical research demonstrates, students are exquisitely sensitive to their teachers' words, thoughts, and deeds. It behooves us to be introspective about our attitudes toward our students.

Drs. Robert Brooks and Sam Goldstein point out that effective educators need to have certain assumptions or mindsets about their roles, which can impact their relationship with students.[31] Some of these assumptions are discussed below.

Realizing the potential for a lifelong impact on your students is imperative

Not to put undue pressure on you, but students watch your every move and take in what you say – and how you say it. This can often tip the balance between whether a student engages in the classroom and the learning process. The author remembers how anxious he was when he had to take a science course in high school. However, he had not counted on having a supportive, warm teacher who instilled a sense of "you can do this" and believed in him. I bought into it and passed the class with flying colors! To this day, I recall her warmth and encouragement.

Attending to the Social/Emotional Life of the Student Is Not an Imposition

Learning does not occur in a vacuum separate from a student's emotions. If we are not feeling optimistic, the chances of student success are limited. No amount of reviewing, re-teaching, or drilling material will be fruitful for a child with learning or emotional difficulties unless the teacher is sensitized to these and communicates their belief in their student.

Research demonstrates that learning is not solely a cognitive process. Instead, learning and feelings go hand in hand, impacting the other. Emotional states such as anxiety, boredom, and annoyance limit a child's learning capacity. While this has been the subject of much research, one study concluded:

> A positive environment puts the brain in the optimal state for learning: minimal stress and maximum interest and engagement with the material to be learned. In large part, this state is created by the teacher with one of the tools for doing so being teacher discourse.[32]

This perspective is especially important for those students with significant learning and emotional challenges. Teachers and school staff need to be aware of students' unique temperamental or dispositional considerations, just as students need to feel secure and self-confident to succeed. Without that security and self-confidence, they will not learn but will instead engage in various competing behaviors that negatively impact their learning and social functioning. This should not be an either/ or situation; we cannot distinguish between curriculum content and a student's emotional life in deciding what to address. Meeting the latter's needs provides the bedrock for the growth of the former. When students experience you as inspiring and believing in them, they will want to work harder to justify that belief.

Feeling a Sense of Partnership with the Teacher and Sharing Responsibility for Classroom Decisions Enhances Student Desire to Learn

Offering students choices when appropriate and encouraging self-expression, even when it might conflict with your perspective, can build a solid relationship. Shared responsibility can go a long way to fostering a sense of ownership, pride, and cooperation in students. In the business world, when employees feel greater involvement and control over what they are doing, they experience greater motivation to meet the needs of their employer and achieve increased satisfaction in their job performance. Students will do the same when presented with similar circumstances.

Showing Appreciation of a Student's Signature Strengths Is Key

Dr. Robert Brooks has coined the term "islands of competence" to illustrate that we all have particular capabilities and assets that should be recognized and utilized. When we identify, reinforce, and employ our students' valuable assets, it significantly enhances their motivation to learn. The first time I meet a student or parent, I inquire about the concerns that brought them to me, but I also make it a point to ask about the child's unique resources. I can then apply these in my work with them. This also conveys to the child that they are not identified solely as having problems but as having something positive and special to offer.

Teachers have a unique opportunity to impact a child's life. On average, a teacher and student are together approximately 1300 hours during an academic year – a vast amount of time that can be utilized for various purposes. In contrast, the amount of quality, uninterrupted time parents spend with their children has been identified to be as low as 38 minutes per day.[33] Parents reported that they are often too busy to set aside time to spend with their children. Twenty-five percent said it is a "daily challenge" to do so given their responsibilities at work, commuting, and other demands such as preparing meals and taking care of the home.[34] This situation may be exacerbated in single parent families. Thus, in many cases, the teacher is the only adult a child can depend on seeing regularly.

The evidence is clear and convincing: When students find themselves in classrooms characterized by warm and engaging relationships with their teachers, they are more willing to persevere in challenging tasks fostering deep learning. These relationships can also act as a buffer against students engaging in negative behaviors. When students experience you as excited to be working with them, it will bring out the best in them, and they want to learn.

In the words of Dr. Robert Brooks, psychologist:

> Teachers should never minimize the role they play in influencing students' lives. Hopefully, that role will be positive, possessing the qualities of a "charismatic adult" who not only touches students' minds, but also their spirits – the way they see and feel about themselves for the rest of their lives. Such influence is truly a rare privilege that should be prized and nurtured.[35]

References

1. Henson, J., Lithgow, J., Goldberg, W., & Nelson, J. (2005). *It's Not Easy Being Green and Other Things to Consider*. Hyperion.
2. Hallowell, E. (2018). *Because I Come from a Crazy Family: The Making of a Psychiatrist*. Bloomsbury.
3. Dwyer, K., Osther, D., & Warger, C. (1999). "Characteristics of a school that is safe and responsive to all children." *Intercultural Development Research Association*. Newsletter, May. www.idra.org/resource-cen ter/characteristics-of-a-school-that-is-safe-and-responsive-to-all-children
4. National Research Council Institute of America. (2004). *Engaging Schools: Fostering High School Students' Motivation to Learn*. The National Academies Press.
5. Murray, C. & Malmgren, K. (2005). "Implementing a teacher-student relationship program in a high-poverty urban school: Effects on social, emotional, and academic adjustment and lessons learned." *Journal of School Psychology* (4392), pp. 137–152.
6. Segal, J. (1988). "Teachers have enormous power in affecting child's self-esteem" in *Child Behavior and Development Letter, Brown University*, 4(10 Oct.), pp 1–3.
7. Ibid.

8. Ibid.

9. Arlen, Harold & Johnny Mercer. (1944). Ac-Cent-Tchu-Ate the Positive. [Various artists]. Los Angeles: Capitol Records.

10. Rosenthal, R. & Jacobson, L. *Pygmalion in the Classroom.* (2003). Crown House Publishing.

11. Ulug, M, Ozden, M. & Eryilmaz, A (2011). "The effects of teachers' attitudes on students' personality and performance." *Procedia – Social and Behavioral Sciences*, 30, pp. 738–742. www.sciencedirect. com/science/article/pii/S1877042811019690?via%3Dihub

12. Blazer, D (2016). *Teacher and Teaching Effects on Students' Academic Performance, Attitudes, and Behaviors.* Doctoral dissertation, Harvard Graduate School of Education. http://nrs.harvard.edu/urn-3:HUL. InstRepos:27112692

    See also: Rashid, M. & Zaman, S. (2016) "Effects of Teacher's Behavior on Academic Performance of Students." Paper presented at 3rd International Conference on Research and Practices in education, At Islamabad, Pakistan. www.researchgate.net/publication/ 325248514_Effects_of_Teacher's_Behavior_on_Academic_Perf ormance_of_Students

    See also Teven, J. & Hanson, T. (2004) "The impact of teacher immediacy and perceived caring on teacher competence and trustworthiness." *Communication Quarterly*, 52(1 Winter), pp. 39–53. https://search.proquest.com/docview/216498235/89786B0 91F904DDBPQ/10?accountid=35022

    See also: Gershenson, S. & Papageorge, N. (2018). "The power of teacher expectations." *Education Next*, 18(1) Retrieved from https:// search.proquest.com/docview/2123679744?accountid=35022

    See also: Sirota, E. & Bailey, L. (2009). "The impact of teachers' expectations on diverse learners' academic outcomes." *Childhood Education*, 85(4), pp. 253–256. Retrieved from https://search.proqu est.com/docview/210394307?accountid=35022

13. Sparks, S. "Why Teacher-Student Relationships Matter." *Education Week.* 3/12/2019. www.edweek.org/teaching-learning/why-teac her-student-relationships-matter/2019/03

14. Bandura, A. (1997) *Self-efficacy: The Exercise of Control.* Worth Publishers.

15. Arzate, H. (2019) "Students who feel they belong are less likely to bully." *Education Week*. www.edweek.org/education/stude nts-who-feel-they-belong-are-less-likely-to-bully-study-finds/ 2019/08

16. Fan, W. & Williams, C. (2010). "The effects of parental involvement on student's academic self-efficacy, engagement, and intrinsic motivation." *Educational Psychology*, 30(1), pp. 53–74.

17. Pajares, F. (1996). "Self-efficacy beliefs in academic settings." *Review of Educational Research*, 66(4), pp. 543–578.

     See also: "Support to student engagement and achievement." *The Journal of School Health*, 74(7 Sept. 2004), pp. 262–273. www. thefreelibrary.com/Relationships+matter%3A+linking+teacher+ support+to+student+engagement...-a0122921722

     See also: Muller, C., Katz, S., & Dance. L. (1999). "Investing in teaching and learning dynamics of the teacher-student relation-ship from each other's perspective." *Urban Education*, 34(3), pp. 292–337.

     See also: Doll, B. (2013) "Enhancing resilience in classrooms," pp. 399– 409 in Goldstein, S. & Brooks, R. (editors), *Handbook of Resilience in Children* – Second Edition. Springer.

18. Alexander, K., Entwisle, D., & Horsey, C. (1997). "From first grade forward: Early foundations of high school dropout." *Sociology of Education*, 70(2), pp. 87–107.

19. Midgley, C., Feldlaufer, H., & Ecacles, J. (1989). "Student/teacher relations and attitudes toward mathematics before and after the transition to junior high school." *Child Development*, 60(4), pp. 981–992.

20. Cataldi, E., Laird, J., & Kewalramani, A. (2009). "High school dropout and completion rates in the United States: 2007" (NCES 2009-064). Washington, DC: National Center for Education Statistics, Institute of Education Sciences, U.S. Department of Education.

21. Dika, S. & Singh, K. (2002). "Applications of social capital in educa-tional literature. A critical synthesis." *Review of Educational Research*, 72(1), pp. 31–60.

22. Alexander, K., Entwisle, D., & Horsey, C. (1997). "From first grade forward: Early foundations of high school dropout." *Sociology of Education*, 70(1), pp. 87–107.

23. Cataldi, E., Laird, J., & Kewalramani, A. (2009). "High school dropout and completion rates in the United States:2007 (NCES 2009-064)." Washington, DC: National Center for Education Statistics, Institute of Education Sciences, U.S. Department of Education.

See also: Midgley, C., Feldlaufer, H., & Ecacles, J. (1989). "Student/teacher relations and attitudes toward mathematics before and after the transition to junior high school." *Child Development*, 60(4), pp. 981–992.

See also: Hughes, J., Cavell, T., & Wilson, V. (2001). "Further support for the developmental significance of the quality of the teacher-student relationship." *Journal of School Psychology*, 39(4) pp. 289–301.

24. Wanders, F, Dijkstra, A, Maslowski, R & van der Veen, V. (2020). "The effect of teacher-student and student-student relationships on the societal involvement of students." *Research Papers in Education*, 35(3), pp. 266–286, DOI: 10.1080/02671522.2019.1568529. www.tandfonline.com/doi/full/10.1080/02671522.2019.1568529

See also: Sparks, S. "Why teacher-student relationships matter." *Education Week.* 3/13/2009. www.edweek.org/teaching-learning/why-teacher-student-relationships-matter/2019/03

25. Schiller, L. & Hinton, C. (2015) "It's true: Happier students get higher grades." *The Conversation,* https://theconversation.com/its-true-happier-students-get-higher-grades-41488

26. Blad, E. (2014) "More than half of students' engaged' in school, says poll." *Education Week.* 4/9/2014. www.edweek.org/leadership/more-than-half-of-students-engaged-in-school-says-poll/2014/04

27. Monitor on Psychology. (2021). vol 52, # 3. *American Psychological Association.* April/May.

28. Sparks, S. (2017) "How teachers' stress affects students: A research roundup." *Education Week.* 7/7/2017. www.edweek.org/education/how-teachers- stress-affects-students-a-research-roundup/2017/06

29. Hagenauer, G., Hascher, T., & Volet, S. (2015). "Teacher emotions in the classroom: Associations with students' engagement, classroom discipline and the interpersonal teacher-student relationship." *European Journal of Psychology of Education*, 30(4), pp. 385–403, Dec. 2015.

30. Ibid.

31. Goldstein S. & Brooks, R. (2007). *Understanding and Managing Children's Classroom Behavior: Creating Sustainable, Resilient Classrooms.* John Wiley & Sons.
32. Podobinska, M. (2017). "Power of teacher's words: the influence on pupil's grades and behavior." *World Scientific News*, 77(1), pp. 1–106.
33. Renner, B. (2018). "American families spend just 37 minutes of quality time together per day, survey find." https://studyfinds.org/american-families-spend-37-minutes-quality-time/
34. Ibid.
35. Brooks, R. (1993). "The impact of teachers: A story of indelible memories and self esteem." www.ldonline.org/ld-topics/teaching-instruction/impact-teachers-story-indelible-memories-and-self-esteem

3

What Is the Strength-Based Model?

Alastor "Mad-eye" Moody, a pure blood wizard in J.K Rowling's *Harry Potter and the Goblet of Fire*, knew how to zero in on Harry's strengths:

> "Play to your strengths."
> "I haven't got any," said Harry before he could stop himself.
> "Excuse me," growled Moody, "you've got strengths if I say you've got them. Think now. What are you best at?"[1]

Mary was a third-grader who resisted efforts by her mother to get her to school on time. Mary told her mother that she "hated" school, refusing to participate in lessons while keeping her head down. Mary also ignored her peers, having little social interaction. She functioned on the fringes of her class.

I consulted with Mary's teacher, and we brainstormed to think of ways we could provide Mary with an incentive to attend school and arrive on time. We came up with the idea of offering Mary a classroom job. The teacher had pointed out that Mary enjoyed being in charge of activities and demonstrated a capacity for organization. I suggested assigning Mary the position of "attendance monitor." Since taking attendance occurred first

DOI: 10.4324/9781003368014-4

thing each morning, this helped ensure that Mary arrived at school on time. Making her responsible for this critical job would tap into her strengths. Mary was given a clipboard with the class roster attached to record daily attendance, reinforcing the idea that she indeed had an "official job."

Mary's mother loved the idea of her daughter having this particular job. However, she was very concerned about Mary's defiant behavior at home. I suggested a "Good Behavior" book for home use in which Mary's parents would keep a daily list of any pro-social behaviors Mary had engaged in during the day. They would review the list with her every night at bedtime.

Mary immediately accepted her classroom job. Within a few days, she became increasingly animated and happy while interacting more frequently with peers. She began arriving at school on time, eager to perform her job, setting a positive tone for the rest of the school day. Her mother shared that there had been a marked improvement in Mary's behavior at home as well. Mary enjoyed talking about being the attendance monitor and took great pleasure in reviewing her daily accomplishments as listed in the good behavior book with her mother, further enhancing their relationship.

These interventions changed Mary's experience both at school and at home from one marked by frustration and disappointment to one of feeling recognized for making a meaningful contribution to the class. Mary's teacher did not present being an attendance monitor as a necessary chore to complete but rather as a request for Mary to help out and contribute. The teacher explicitly communicated to Mary that she was a valued member of the class with something to offer while also instilling a sense of responsibility and greater connection to the school. It is not surprising that Mary responded immediately and positively. In addition, Mary found the task to be fun, which was self-reinforcing, leading to increased interaction with peers.

This vignette captures the essence of the strength-based model and illustrates how it can be utilized in school efficiently. Even better – this intervention did not cost a penny to implement! When I initially approached the teacher, I could have focused on Mary's deficits and tried to help improve her attention span or teach her better social skills. While there could be merit in such an approach, and many would advocate for it, I decided to work with Mary's natural ability to organize and carry out a task that interested her. By suggesting a task that utilized her well-developed skills, the wheel did not have to be reinvented. Mary was highly motivated to take on this responsibility, and the rest was history!

As illustrated in this example, the strength-based model is not the only way to conceptualize the challenges people experience. Psychiatrist R.D. Laing has coined the term "medical model" to denote how physical illness was viewed, diagnosed and treated.[2] In the medical model, the physician focuses on dysfunction and uses a problem-solving approach to diagnose and devise a treatment plan. The physician obtains a medical history, conducts a physical examination, and performs diagnostic tests to help identify and then treat a specific illness.

The medical model has been a boon to the treatment and eradication of many physical diseases and, over the years, has become the primary way to conceptualize illness in the Western Hemisphere. However, recent approaches such as holistic medicine and treatment modalities from other cultures have gained popularity in the West.

Initially, the medical model was also used to identify and treat mental illness. As the medical model assumes that illness has biological and genetic determinants, this influenced the early views of mental illness. Sigmund Freud's creation of psychoanalysis and pioneering use of what he called the "talking cure," along with the work of other psychoanalysts, was one of the earliest attempts to treat mental illness as a psychological phenomenon. Treating deficits and eradicating symptoms was the primary focus of psychological treatment.

In the 20th century, other models to explain human behavior gained popularity. In 1943, psychologist Abraham Maslow proposed a hierarchy of human needs ranging from food, water, and sex, to the need to self-actualize or achieve one's full potential. Although psychologists questioned the methodology used to develop this theory, it was an early attempt to conceptualize human growth as positive.[3] Maslow helped popularize a school of thought called Humanistic Psychology. For Maslow,

> The science of psychology has been far more successful on the negative than on the positive side; it has revealed to us much about man's shortcomings, his illnesses, his sins, but little about his potentialities, his virtues, his achievable aspirations, or his full psychological height. It is as if psychology had voluntarily restricted itself to only half its rightful jurisdiction, and that the darker, meaner half.[4]

This was a radical idea in the field of psychology at the time. Instead of focusing on how to remediate symptoms, the idea of helping people flourish was proposed.

In the 1950s, psychologist Robert White wrote that sex and aggression, drives at the cornerstone of the psychoanalytic model, could not alone account for varied human behaviors such as playfulness and exploration.[5] White proposed that people had an intrinsic need for competence and knowledge about interacting with their environment effectively. If these needs are not met, it can lead to a lack of fulfillment, but if such behaviors lead to success, they promote efficacy and pleasure, and we are motivated to continue these behaviors.

Despite these early attempts to view human development as governed by a need for positive growth, it was not until the 1980s that the positive psychology movement kick-started. In a speech before the American Psychological Association, Dr. Martin Seligman spoke about the emphasis in psychology on mental illness and its remediation.[6] While understanding this was necessary to provide treatment, Seligman noted that other areas were neglected, such as promoting optimal functioning. Thus, much of what is adaptive about people was under-examined. As Seligman pointed out, psychologists

> Have discovered that there is a set of human strengths that are the most likely buffers against mental illness: courage, optimism, interpersonal skill, work ethic, hope, honesty,

and perseverance. Much of the task of prevention will be to create a science of human strength whose mission will be to foster these virtues in young people.[7]

This was a continuation of Maslow's ideas from many years earlier.

Following Seligman's challenge for psychology to become invested in identifying and utilizing a person's strengths to enhance their life, the field of positive psychology was born. Seligman defines positive psychology as "the scientific study of the strengths that enable individuals and communities to thrive. The field is founded on the belief that people want to lead meaningful and fulfilling lives, to cultivate what is best within themselves, and to enhance their experiences of love, work, and play."[8]

Since Seligman's landmark address, positive psychology has become a legitimate field of study. As a result, psychology has come full circle with the study and understanding of human strengths given as much credence today as the study of mental illness was in the past. Utilizing strengths, enhancing resilience, and promoting happiness are now regarded as legitimate areas to study and achieve.

Viewing people through the lens of a deficit model implies that they have a problem that can negatively distinguish them from others and define them. This model typically leads the professional to take charge of the problem and focus on what the person supposedly lacks. This response prevents the person who has the "problem" from controlling it and learning from it effectively. While we do not want to deny or minimize challenges, focusing primarily on them creates a sense of hopelessness and does not generally empower the person seeking help. In a strength-based model, we can identify and utilize the resources of the person to address challenges.

The strength-based model opens us up to new opportunities. Instead of putting teachers and clinicians in the roles of fixers, it allows us to become facilitators; we work with individual children or families to help them discover the unique resources within them. Rather than having these resources ignored, as in the medical model of psychotherapy, we utilize them as allies in the child's quest for development. Believing you can jumpstart the process of a child using resources that they may or may not even be aware they possess is a potent gift.

Experiencing obstacles as challenges to embrace rather than avoid is a powerful mindset to instill. In using a strength-based model, we do not ignore them, but rather, along with the child, seek to confront and master them. This awakens students as well as teachers, clinicians, and parents to the process of change that occurs within the child. In this way, children become active agents of change in meeting their goals.

Another example of utilizing a positive psychology framework occurred when I was introduced to a sixth-grader named Peter, a bright, verbal youngster who suffered from obsessive-compulsive disorder (OCD). Among Peter's symptoms was a tendency to engage in overthinking various topics (obsessive thoughts) to the point of tuning out events going on around him. This impacted his functioning in various situations, one of which concerned him more than any other – his performance on the neighborhood soccer team. Peter enjoyed being on the team, however, his repetitive extraneous thoughts limited his ability to comply with the demands of practicing and playing the game. To an observer, it would appear that Peter was bored and disinterested, as he appeared very distracted. In reality, he was very attuned to his thoughts and focused intently on them, although this did not help him on the soccer field.

In discussing this with Peter, he shared that he was very stressed about how his obsessive thinking was putting his position on the team at risk. As we talked, I recognized that this symptom did not necessarily have to be viewed by him as a deficit to be eliminated. I pointed out to Peter that one of the OCD symptoms he presented with, hypervigilance, the state of being extremely alert or watchful, could be channeled to his advantage on the field. Instead of his attention being drawn by extraneous things around him, such as looking to see who was in the stands or watching birds fly, that same tendency could be used to follow the path of the ball. I conveyed to Peter that being able to hyper-focus was a gift rather than a problem, and learning how to channel it could make him a better soccer player. Peter was very excited about this change in his mindset. Instead, what was previously viewed as a challenge could be experienced as an asset. Peter and I came up with self-directed verbal cues he could use in a game to help keep his focus on the ball. By reframing a challenge as a strength, Peter's self-esteem grew, and as his performance on the field improved, his passion for playing the game also grew. Over time Peter developed an exceptional ability to follow the path of a ball and became the goalie for this team. By allowing Peter to view his obsessive thinking as an asset to embrace and utilize rather than a deficit to eradicate, he was able to sharpen his focus to the point where nothing else existed but the ball.

One area that has been researched a great deal in the strength-based model is the topic of resilience. One of the giants of this field is psychologist Dr. Ann Masten who has studied this topic extensively and provides the following useful definition of resilience.

> The word resilience stems from the Latin verb *resilire* (to rebound). In colloquial English, the word resiliency retains a similar meaning, referring to the property of elasticity or springing back, much as a rubber band does after it is stretched and then released. A human individual could be described as resilient when showing a pattern of adaptation or recovery in the context of potentially destabilizing threats.[9]

In her extensive studies of this topic, Masten concluded: "Resilience does not come from rare and special qualities, but from the everyday magic of ordinary, normative human resources in the minds, brains, and bodies of children, in their families and their communities."[10]

This conclusion has significant ramifications. Empirical evidence confirms that resilience is not an unusual phenomenon reserved for a select few possessed with an incredible intellectual or emotional endowment. Instead, it is a quality whose gifts are available to all. Rather than looking at children through the prism of their deficits, we need to design interventions that incorporate their strengths and assets while not ignoring their vulnerabilities or possible risk factors.

As mentioned previously, Drs. Robert Brooks and Sam Goldstein are considered leaders in this field and have authored several books and articles on resiliency. Many of their concepts will be shared throughout this book. Their collaboration has championed the idea that utilizing this model should not be reserved only for at-risk children. The ideals can be applied to all children who can benefit from the principles of a strength-based approach.[11] This is consistent with Seligman's idea of positive psychology being used to improve the quality of life for all by helping people flourish.

While strength-based practices have been used extensively by mental health practitioners, the beauty of this model is that it can be efficiently utilized by educators, parents, and coaches. Children and their families can be viewed as having the strengths, resources, and ability to bounce back from adversity. As described by Hammond:

> A strength-based paradigm offers a different language to describe children's and families' difficulties and struggles. It allows one to see opportunities, hope, and solutions rather than just problems and hopelessness …This fundamental shift means working with and facilitating rather than fixing, pointing to health rather than dysfunction, turning away from limiting labels and diagnosis to wholeness and well-being. Embracing a strength-based paradigm encourages seeing beyond the risk behaviors and characteristics of children, youth, and families in high-need communities to the potential of what can be.[12]

Some of the principles of a strength-based orientation have been outlined by Hammond.[13]

- ◆ An absolute belief that every person has potential, and it is these unique strengths and capabilities, not their limitations, that will determine their evolving story as well as define who they are.
- ◆ What we focus on becomes our reality. By focusing on strengths, not labels, we can see challenges as

opportunities rather than something to avoid. This creates hope and optimism.

◆ Be aware of the assumptions and beliefs you have about students, as this impacts your interactions with them.

◆ The language we use creates reality for care providers, children, and their families.

◆ A belief that change is inevitable – all individuals have the urge to succeed, explore the world around them, and make themselves useful to others and their communities.

◆ Positive change occurs in the context of authentic relationships – people need to know someone cares for them unconditionally and will be there in a time of need. Caring about others is a transactional and facilitating process supporting change and enhancing capabilities. The relationships we have with students can inspire them to great heights.

Essentially, the positive psychology model allows children to access and apply their assets in their endeavors both in and out of the classroom.

References

1. Rowling, J.K. (2005). *Harry Potter and the Goblet of Fire*. Bloomsbury.
2. Laing, R.D. (1998). *Politics of The Family and Other Essays*. Routledge.
3. Maslow, A. (2018). *Theory of Human Motivation*. Wilder.
4. Ibid.
5. White, R. (1959). Motivation Reconsidered: The Concept Of Competence. *Psychological Review*, 66(5 Sept.), pp. 297–333.
6. Seligman, M.E. (1999). President's Address from The APA 1998 Annual Report. *American Psychologist*, 54, pp. 559–562.
7. Ibid.
8. Positive Psychology Center of the University of Pennsylvania. (2022). Pennsylvania State University Positive Psychology Program www.ppc.sas.upenn.edu
9. Masten, A. (2014). *Ordinary Magic: Resilience in Development*. Guilford Press.

10. Ibid.
11. Brooks, R. & Goldstein, S. (2002). *Raising Resilient Children*. McGraw-Hill.
12. Hammond, W. (2010). "Principles of strength-based practice." Resiliency Initiatives.
13. Ibid.

4

How to Apply the Strength-Based Model in the Classroom

Who better than the recipient of a state teacher of the year award, to understand the importance of building good relationships with students? James Ford, 2015 North Carolina state teacher of the year puts it this way:

> The relational part of teaching may very well be its most underrated aspect. When teachers are good at building relationships with students, the skill is seen more as a cover for lack of content knowledge or wherewithal to instruct with rigor. Our first job as teachers is make sure that we teach our students, that we connect with them on a real level, showing respect for their culture and affirming their worthiness to receive the best education possible.[1]
>
> James Ford
> 2015 North Carolina State Teacher of the Year

Research in positive psychology has identified many interventions that enhance resilience in students, many of which will be examined in this and the next chapter. These ideas come to life when students experience them with a safe and trusted adult who expresses a sense of caring encouragement, conveying to a child how valued they are.

DOI: 10.4324/9781003368014-5

Mindsets

Steve Maraboli, decorated military veteran, philanthropist, and creator of empowerment and literacy programs in over 40 countries worldwide, points out the importance of mindset for change.

> Once your mindset changes, everything on the outside will change along with it.[2]

A mythical story tells of two travelers who separately came across a farmer while passing through the mountains. The first traveler approached the farmer, asked for directions to the next town, and then wanted to know if the farmer could tell him what the people in that town were like. In response, the farmer asked the traveler what the people were like in the town he had just left. The traveler replied that the people were awful – they spoke an unfamiliar language, made him sleep on a cold floor, fed him an unfamiliar food that tasted terrible, and added that he hoped he never had to go back there. The farmer replied that the people in the next town would be no different. The traveler resumed his walk.

Later, another traveler approached the farmer, asked for directions to the next town, and inquired about the people who lived there. The farmer asked him what the people in the previous town were like. The traveler replied that the inhabitants were wonderful. Even though they spoke a language he didn't understand, they had treated him very kindly and fed him their traditional food, which was different from anything he had tasted before. It was cold and he had to sleep on the floor, but he was given blankets, and the people tried their best to help him stay warm. He liked it there so much that he did not want to leave. The farmer told the traveler, just as he had told the previous one, that the people in the next town were no different.[3]

The vignette illustrates how powerful our thoughts can be in evaluating a situation. The first traveler demonstrated a negative mindset, while the second illustrated a positive mindset. How we interpret events impacts our experience of them, as well as our emotions and expectations.

The assumptions we make about others, our world, and ourselves affect how we respond to events and understand the actions of others. Suppose you believe that a student cannot do well in class or will struggle mightily. Students will inevitably pick up on this. Your expectations will become a self-fulfilling prophecy for that student, as demonstrated in the study by Rosenthal discussed in the last chapter. How we understand and react to a student's attempts to gain mastery of a task or concept is crucial. Psychologist Dr. Carol Dweck has been instrumental in researching how student mindset impacts how they experience setbacks and their self-image.

Dweck conducted a series of experiments in which children were given identical easy puzzle tasks to complete. Following this, they were randomly divided into two groups. Each child was given a numerical score and then given one sentence of feedback. In one group, the students were told how smart they were to complete the task, while students in the other group were complimented on how hard they tried. The students were then allowed to choose either another easy task or a much more difficult one they were told would be very interesting to complete. The overwhelming majority of the "smart" group picked another easy puzzle task, while the vast majority of the students complimented on their effort picked the more difficult task. Thus, most of the so-called "smart" children gave up. When both groups were assigned a challenging puzzle task, the "effort" group worked diligently, attempting novel solutions, and said they enjoyed working on the puzzle. However, the "smart" group was visibly agitated and gave up. These particular children experienced their failure as a confirmation of a lack of intelligence.[4]

Dweck's research suggested that those who feel innate intelligence is the main ingredient to success will be more likely to play down the importance of effort, believing that intelligence alone will carry them through to a successful result. The students in the "smart" group in Dweck's study have characteristics of what is referred to as a fixed mindset.

A fixed mindset holds that intelligence is set from birth with a finite amount, and any degree of effort or future learning cannot alter that amount. Talent, rather than effort, is believed to be the key to success. Students with a fixed mindset experience making a mistake as overwhelming and believe it validates their belief that they lack intelligence.

In contrast, a growth mindset holds that intelligence can be further developed through effort and hard work. The skills present at birth are just the beginning; making mistakes provides an opportunity to learn and improve. The students in the Dweck study who eagerly took on the more challenging puzzle task exhibited this growth mindset and were more willing to take a risk.

The mindset our students present will undoubtedly impact how much effort they will exert in the classroom and, on a deeper level, influence how they feel about themselves and how high they set their aspirations. Will they be learners who view setbacks as opportunities to learn? Or will they avoid learning situations in which they risk committing errors and not try due to fear of failure or looking bad in the eyes of others or themselves?

Dweck's research demonstrates how exquisitely sensitive children are to the words of an educator. The statements we make to students profoundly impact how they view themselves, how they behave, and what they believe they can accomplish. "Be mindful when it comes to your words. Some that do not mean much to you may stick with someone else for a lifetime,"[5] says Rachel Wolchin, a teacher and writer. What we say to our students can stick to them like glue.

To promote a growth mindset, it is essential to communicate to students that it is not the outcome, grade, or overall level of success that primarily interests us. Instead, it is the effort they put into a task. Effort is a variable that students can control, but we need to provide practical encouragement to teach them how to exert appropriate effort and channel it to achieve their best outcome. Below is a collection of statements that promote a growth mindset.

An important point is that we should avoid telling students how smart they are. While there is a natural tendency to do this, the message children internalize when hearing this is that "smarts" matter, and anything that threatens them, such as taking risks and making mistakes, should be avoided.

Below are statements that can be used by a teacher to promote the development of a growth mindset for students. These statements emphasize effort, perseverance, creativity, and attitude over natural intelligence. These statements can be reinforcing to a child who is struggling with an unachievable desire to be perfect.

One example of a situation is offering immediate feedback to a student as they are working on a task. For instance, as you observe students complete an assignment in the classroom, you can note how the students are working. Some specific examples of feedback in that situation can be:

♦ I can tell you are really trying hard.
♦ I like the effort you are putting into that.
♦ I like the way you are doing that (you can be specific as you like and can add comments such as great handwriting, you are really organized, etc.).
♦ That's a really original approach to solving that problem.
♦ I can see that hard problems don't scare you off.
♦ Wow! You came up with that all on your own.

Another instance to use these statements can be directed to students upon the completion of a project, unit, or at the end of a marking period or semester:

♦ You stuck with it even when it got really difficult.
♦ Look how much you have improved over the past semester. You should be proud and give yourself a pat on the back.
♦ I like the way you were a team player on that group project.
♦ Wow! You must have studied really hard for this test.
♦ You put in your best effort and it shows.
♦ You're not afraid to tackle the hard stuff.

Fostering a growth mindset does not only have to pertain to academic tasks. In addition, these remarks can be applied to social or group situations:

♦ You worked well with everyone on that group project.
♦ It is nice the way you get along with your classmates.
♦ I noticed you helped _____ (fill in name of student) on the project. That was so nice of you.
♦ I appreciate how you helped out today when _____ _____ (teacher can fill in the blank as appropriate such as tidying up the room, working on the bulletin board, or doing a classroom job).
♦ I love how involved you were in class today.
♦ Your contribution to the group project made it even better.
♦ It's great how you give others a chance to contribute.
♦ I loved how supportive you are of your classmates.

Finally, these statements can be targeted to promote organizational skills:

♦ I love your can-do attitude.
♦ I love how you tackled that assignment.
♦ Specific behavioral statements such as, you got a great sense of humor, you are a really hard worker, or you are very organized.
♦ That was very mature of you.
♦ You managed that situation with a lot of maturity.
♦ You weren't afraid to take on that assignment.
♦ You are always ready for class – that's great!
♦ Your workspace always looks so neat.
♦ Good job remembering your _____ today (can range from homework to lunch money and everything in-between).
♦ You took the time to check your work. That's great! (Or any other skill, such as proofreading or not being tardy).
♦ Great choice – good decision on that!

In addition to teachers promoting these messages, students can be taught self-affirmations to reinforce their self-confidence. For instance, self-talk statements that students can use while working on a task can include:

- I learn and grow from my mistakes.
- I will keep trying until I figure this out.
- I am getting there.
- I'm not afraid to try hard problems.
- This can take a while and I will stick with it.
- I don't give up.
- I can tell I am making progress.
- I don't let myself get down when it gets hard.
- Hard stuff doesn't scare me.
- I keep trying.
- I am not embarrassed to ask for help.
- I don't compare myself to others.
- I can't do it – yet. I am going to keep trying.

Examples of self-affirmations that students can make about themselves or their schoolwork can include:

- I want to succeed.
- I am good at coming up with solutions.
- I am not scared of new things.
- I am not afraid of a challenge. I take them on.
- I'm brave.
- If I were a superhero, my power would be learning.
- I never give up.
- I want to learn.

Finally, statements that students can make that are self-congratulatory can include:

- I like to try hard things.
- Practice makes me better.

- ◆ My brain gets bigger and stronger when I learn new things.
- ◆ I like to try new ways to solve problems.
- ◆ I'm a learner.
- ◆ Learning new things is cool.

Feedback is an essential part of teaching. In fact, every day, we are almost constantly providing feedback to students and parents in countless ways, not just verbally. Our body language, the volume and tone of voice, as well as our facial expressions convey meaning to the listener.

In delivering feedback to students from a strength-based perspective, it is helpful to use growth mindset principles. As noted earlier, it is essential to focus on student effort rather than just outcome. The feedback should be encouraging and affirming whether the student performed well on the task or not. Focus on what the student may have done well and point out how they can build upon it by enlarging their repertoire of ways to respond. When there are errors, point them out to the student as opportunities to learn. If a student believes their error will help them learn, they will be more engaged in the task and less fearful of making mistakes.

Do not merely comment on the student's answer, especially if it was incorrect – encourage student introspection. For instance, help them understand the mental processes they used in coming up with their answer ("What made you decide to try that method?"), how they can improve ("What do you think you can do differently next time?"), and what they took away from their mistakes ("When X occurred, how did you feel and what did you learn from it?"). This type of feedback encourages student self-evaluation, as they will more fully understand how they attempted to solve the problem.

Feedback in a strength-based approach does not simply identify weaknesses and encourage the student to try again. Instead, this type of feedback utilizes student talents and resources to address the weakness. The student is asked to consider how these resources can be used to improve the quality of their work, grades, and test performance. We want students to understand that their strengths are the best way to overcome deficits. Feedback delivered in this manner can help students feel empowered and take concrete action to meet their goals.

Teaching children to think independently about how to be successful and happy while nurturing a love of learning is one of the most precious gifts we can give our students. In addition to the methods cited here, a plethora of other resources devised to promote growth mindsets can be found online and are commercially available for teachers and parents.

Intrinsic versus Extrinsic Motivation

Academy award-winning graphic designer and film maker, Saul Bass, said

I want to make beautiful things, even if nobody cares.[6]

Bass, who designed opening movie credits for Hitchcock's Psycho, Scorsese's Goodfellas, and even the AT&T logo, was describing intrinsic human motivation.

Closely aligned with the concept of growth mindsets is fostering intrinsic motivation within students. This concept grew out of the research of two psychologists, Dr. Richard Ryan and Dr. Edward Deci.

Drs. Ryan and Deci attempted to explain human motivation by examining how "social-contextual factors can either promote or inhibit people's thriving through the satisfaction of their basic psychological needs for competence, relatedness, and autonomy."[7] The model Ryan and Deci formulated, "Self Determination Theory" (SDT), is an optimistic view of human motivation. It attempts to identify those environmental variables that allow us to thrive.

One of the most important contributions of SDT is the notion of intrinsic versus extrinsic motivation. Ryan and Deci provide the following definition for these concepts.

Intrinsically motivated behaviors are those that are performed out of self-interest and for which the primary reward is "spontaneous feelings of effectance and enjoyment that accompany the behaviors."[8] Thus, reading a novel, practicing your backhand, or performing volunteer work are all examples of intrinsically motivated behavior. It makes us feel good to do it, so we engage in it and feel we are getting something out of it. In contrast, extrinsic motivation is represented by a behavior that is instrumental for a positive consequence. Ryan and Deci define this as "an external reward or social approval, avoidance of punishment, or the attainment of a valued outcome."[9]

Engaging in a task for a tangible reward, such as a child doing household chores to earn their allowance, or doing a favor to obtain a reward, are examples of extrinsically motivated behavior. A child putting away their toys or simply helping someone without prompting, payment, or reward are examples of intrinsically motivated behavior. Environmental factors control extrinsically motivated behaviors; intrinsically motivated behaviors originate from within us.

This research has implications within the classroom. While there are certainly students who respond to external rewards and interventions such as charts and stickers, evidence reveals that working to experience a sense of inner satisfaction and feeling a sense of accomplishment produces longer-lasting motivation. Internal motivation propels us to explore, play and learn, and maintain the desire to do so rather than engaging in such activities for an external reward. A large body of research confirms the phenomenon of externally administered rewards reducing intrinsic motivation.[10] For instance, if I enjoy baking and giving away my goods to friends and family for no other reason than simply because I want to, this would be intrinsic motivation at work. However, if people began paying me for the baked goods, the inherent satisfaction I originally had would dissipate over time, and the experience would not be as fulfilling as it had been before a profit motive became a factor.

In addition, when external rewards are given for specific behaviors, such as reading, the evidence is that we tend to overvalue the reward while losing enthusiasm for the process used to achieve it. Providing external rewards for classroom behavior can actually reduce motivation. Parents who pay their children to study or get good grades will achieve the goal of heightening their child's interest in money while lowering their motivation to learn. Similar findings have also been seen in the business world.[11] This finding highlights the difference between extrinsic and intrinsic motivation, two very different processes. It is crucial to consider the type of motivation we are reinforcing to develop a child's love for learning rather than the reward waiting for them. Students focused primarily on grades and rewards will be less inclined to examine creative ways to solve problems but will want the easiest way to collect their reward. The question becomes how to foster the growth of intrinsic motivation in students.[12]

One way to boost intrinsic motivation in students is to offer them the opportunity for input about what they will be learning. This does not necessarily mean you give them total control over the content to be presented – limit the choices so you can teach the required curriculum effectively. However, the simple act of allowing input boosts intrinsic motivation for students and communicates to them that you value their involvement, making them active partners in the learning process. As discussed in previous chapters, people of all ages tend to be more interested in things they play a part in choosing.

Prioritizing content mastery and understanding concepts presented instead of test scores also helps children appreciate learning and increase their desire to learn. It is also helpful to understand student needs and get to know their concerns so material can, where possible and appropriate, be tailored to be more relevant to their lives. Structuring assignments to incorporate student interests will increase their desire to learn the material.

When student curiosity is piqued, they will be more likely to want to learn about a subject. Explore this with your students. Ask them what it is about the content that has been presented that interests them enough to want to learn more about it. Work together with your student to help them find something about a particular assignment that resonates with them.

Finally, model intrinsic motivation by sharing some of your interests with your students. Demonstrating your love of learning to your students will help stimulate their enthusiasm to learn. I recall working with a student who was struggling with physics. He was also on the school baseball team, so I shared with him that I was intrigued by an exhibit I had seen at a museum about how physics was applied to the "science" of throwing and hitting a baseball. This captured his attention. Pointing him toward where he could find information about this subject helped him begin to see the relevance of the material in class – physics – to something he already cared about and was interested in – baseball. His attitude toward physics changed, and a healthy curiosity emerged with him approaching the subject by wanting to understand it more fully.

Fear of Making Mistakes

Very few inventors know more about failure than Thomas Edison who ultimately found success with the invention of the electric light bulb.

> I have not failed. I just found 10,000 ways that won't work.[13]

Nothing is as intimidating as fear of complete failure or making a mistake. This potent stressor can hold people back in so many ways that it robs them of the opportunity to take risks, grow, and learn, let alone succeed. I have vivid memories as an athletically challenged child who feared striking out or dropping the ball. My fear was so pervasive that I would lie to my gym teachers, telling them I "forgot" my gym uniform that day and thus was unprepared for PE class and would have to sit out the activities. I was willing to take the unprepared grade for the day rather than risk a poor performance on the baseball field or basketball court.

A recent study found that students who internalized fear of failure at an early age were less likely to work toward developing and nurturing their interests. They were also less likely to use effective learning strategies and had a higher probability of engaging in cheating behaviors, which may eventually turn into a negative cycle.[14] Students who rely on cheating may dismiss positive feedback from their teacher as they attribute their success to cheating rather than ability.

I recall treating a fourth-grade boy referred for therapy by his parents due to his extreme shyness. Over time he grew to trust me and began talking about his school performance. He was a competent student yet was receiving low grades. He finally acknowledged that he intentionally avoided classroom discussion, even though he knew the answers. He would also complete assignments and tests with the minimal amount of information he could, choosing not to elaborate. When queried about this, he admitted that his fear of making a mistake was monumental. He would purposely hold back responses to questions in class as he feared being judged harshly by peers and teachers if he was incorrect. He understood how this held him back from being the best student he could be, but his fear of making an error was overwhelming.

The fear of making mistakes is palpable even on a neurological level. Neuroscientists have found that mistakes set off a chain of events in our brain. Specific neurons are aware of our mistakes even before we are consciously aware we have made them. When we make a mistake, these neurons immediately fire, activating our brain's fear center – this is "the same fear center that lights up when people see snakes or spiders,"[15] impeding its ability to problem-solve. Fortunately, our brain encodes contradictory information to foster more effective problem-solving skills in these situations.[16]

This emotion is readily apparent in the classroom. How many students avoid contributing to class discussions as they fear being embarrassed and negatively evaluated by their peers and teachers? I suspect the number is very high. Too many children view an error as a commentary on or confirmation of their incompetence. The goal is to help students view errors as opportunities that can go a long way to cementing a positive connection with you and the material. How can we accomplish this?

Teachers play a critical role in this process. The classroom culture needs to convey that school is a place to learn new information, problem-solve, receive correct answers, experience both success and failure – and bounce back. Teachers can explicitly convey to their students how to learn from their own experiences, and one of the best ways to do that is to include the opportunity to learn what went wrong. Students need to understand that mistakes are part of the growth and learning process and, in the long run, can serve to make them better students. Point out that wrong answers shed more light on the subject and help us understand the topic even better than when the correct answer was offered in the first instance.

Working to create a mindset in the classroom that failure and errors are part of life and represent an opportunity to improve at something is an essential objective for every teacher. This can begin on the first day of school, as outlined by Dr. Robert Brooks. Teachers usually use that time to set the tone for the year, and it is a perfect opportunity to bring this point front and center for your students. For instance, you can ask the class if anyone is afraid to make a mistake. Before anyone has an opportunity to raise their hand (which most students will be reluctant to do), your hand should be the first one to go up. At that point, you can share an example of a mistake you have made and what you learned from it. This communicates that mistakes are everyday occurrences that can happen to anyone – even the teacher! It helps create a class mindset about the role mistakes play in the classroom and validates the concept that they are a part of real, everyday life. Starting the school year this way can lead to a classroom discussion, with students brainstorming about how to support each other. This will include treating peers with respect when they make a mistake – after all, it is inevitable.

Recently, a study compared how math teachers from the United States and China reacted to their students' mistakes. The teachers from the United States would often respond by correcting their students' errors, which the researchers concluded would fuel fear of failure because students feared looking incompetent. In contrast, the teachers from China were more open and relaxed about the freedom to make mistakes. The investigators concluded that these teachers were more effective in creating a mistake-friendly environment. Errors were seen as regular events and destigmatized, making the students more open to correcting their mistakes. The inevitability of making mistakes was modeled for these students.[17]

In addition to creating a class mindset that says that mistakes are acceptable, you can utilize the following strategies to help students feel less ashamed and angry with themselves for committing an error.

- ◆ Do not mark errors on tests without explaining what was wrong with the answer. I know a teacher who never used red ink to highlight a mistake on a paper or test. Instead, she would use green ink to indicate a mistake. She would tell her students that green is for go and growth and red is for stop and angry.

- ◆ Provide students with opportunities to correct mistakes and redo their work; making mistakes becomes an opportunity to learn.

- ◆ If a student makes a mistake during class discussion, do not respond by saying, "that is incorrect. Who else has an answer?" Instead, ask the student why they think that is the correct response and ask them to provide an example to support their reasoning.

- ◆ Have students post their biggest mistakes on a bulletin board to "brag" about them – after the teacher posts a mistake of their own first. You can also ask students to list a ridiculous mistake they have made or even be creative and make up a pretend mistake to avoid feeling vulnerable when sharing a real one.

- ◆ Cite examples from history, entertainment, or pop culture of mistakes well-known people made and how they worked out. In contrast, you can have a class discussion of when people ridiculed particular inventions or historical events. The purchase of Alaska from Russia in 1867 was ridiculed as "Seward's Folly" as it was thought the Secretary of State who arranged it, William Seward, had bought nothing but a giant iceberg. Even the Beatles, the greatest rock group of all time, were turned down by a record company executive who explained to their manager, "groups with guitars are on the way out."

◆ Modeling persistence for your students in the face of challenges is a powerful way to encourage them to engage in similar behaviors. A study in which adults modeled such behavior toward meeting a goal influenced children as young as 15 months old to mimic them.[18] Persistence can be learned, so it should be modeled.

◆ Just as persistence can be modeled, so can self-compassion. It is beneficial for students to witness you being understanding and accepting of any shortcomings or errors you have made. The message students can learn is not to hold themselves to unrealistically high standards, understanding that if – actually when – they slip up in the future, they can react in a non-punitive manner. It also shows students that they are not alone in dealing with setbacks.

◆ If a student gives an incorrect answer, you should go beyond just saying "no." Rather than merely commenting about the incorrect response, explain why the answer was wrong. Then redo the problem to demonstrate how to get to the correct answer. You could even try another example to reinforce the process.

◆ Search for any semblance of the correct response in a wrong answer. Instead, encourage the student to see if they can also discover this. Sometimes, wrong responses may be totally off base, but they can also be slightly amiss. With a gentle nudge, a student can see this.

◆ An incorrect response offered by a student can allow for a class discussion as other students analyze the response. The entire class can benefit from the incorrect response if the discussion is done respectfully.

◆ Acknowledge to the student that how they arrived at the answer is often more interesting than the answer itself. Most answers are born following a period of thought. How did the student arrive at this response? Was it too hastily? Was the question simply misread or misheard? What was the thinking that went into it? Try tapping into this with a student when they make a mistake. Considering these questions helps you discover if the error was due to a lack of understanding or other factors.

◆ An idea to share with your students is that even brilliant people can be wrong as scientists go through trial and error. Additionally, scientists try everything they can to prove themselves wrong, ensuring that the results are as accurate as possible. Each of us benefits each time someone is wrong.

Studies that assessed how resilient people respond to making mistakes found that individuals with higher self-esteem were not perfectionists. They could explain their errors in a positive, non-defensive manner and bounce back quickly.[19]

For young children, stories such as *The Little Engine That Could*,[20] *After the Fall (How Humpty Dumpty Got Back Up Again)*,[21] and *Rosie Revere, Engineer*,[22] all teach that failure does not define us but is a step that can facilitate growth.

Making mistakes needs to be encouraged, and students need to feel allowed to fail. As discussed earlier, mistakes can be great stepping-stones to what comes next. Failure can make us more compassionate and provides us with an opportunity to rethink how we do things, increasing our chances of success by pointing us to new strategies to achieve our goals. Communicating this to students and encouraging them to take risks can be incredibly liberating.

I recall two vignettes demonstrating how a child can deal with a mistake. Once, when I was at my son's little league baseball game, one of the children struck out with the bases loaded. It ended the game, and his team lost. He immediately threw his bat down and screamed at the umpire for what he perceived as a "botched" call. The boy stomped back to the dugout, threw down his helmet, kicked the water container, and started to cry. I felt bad for this boy and wondered how he handled disappointments in other areas of his life.

In contrast, a student I saw in counseling had learning challenges and was anxious about an upcoming exam. Although he diligently prepared for it, he failed nonetheless. His reaction was to seek out the teacher, but rather than complaining about the test or lobbying for a higher grade, he reviewed the questions he missed to understand his mistakes. These were two very different reactions to failure that had implications for how resilient these children would be in different scenarios in their lives both inside and outside the classroom.

I am reminded of a 12-year-old student I will call "James," whom I saw in school-based counseling. James was diagnosed as being on the autism spectrum and quickly lost his temper when frustrated by schoolwork. One day his teacher brought him to my office after he had an outburst in class. When James was calm, I asked him what happened, and he explained that he had made a mistake on an art project and felt the entire project was ruined.

James was distraught, and as he relayed the episode and I was thinking about how to respond to him from a strength-based framework, I had an outside-of-the-box idea. I took out a pencil, held it up, and asked James what I was holding. He smiled (which was already an improvement from his earlier behavior), and when he correctly responded, I asked what the thing on the top of the pencil was called. He replied, "an eraser," giving me a look of confusion. I replied, "Pencils have erasers because people are expected to make mistakes. That is part of learning anything new. That's why they were invented!"

James began to cry, saying how horrible he was in art. I asked how hard he had tried, and he said he put in a great deal of effort on the project. I told him that as long as he tried, he could always be proud, and in this case, he had tried very hard. At his point, James reminded me of a story I had previously shared with him about Willie Stargell, a Hall of Famer baseball player who was an outstanding hitter but had also accumulated a large number of strikeouts. Stargell had once remarked, "I'm proud of my strikeouts too, for I feel that to succeed, one must first fail; and the more you fail, the more you learn about succeeding."[23] Stargell's setbacks as a hitter ultimately contributed to his success. I shared with James that I was very impressed that he remembered that story. He said he would take the picture home to show his parents even though it included his mistake.

The next day when school started, James showed up at my office very excited, wanting to show me a PowerPoint presentation he had made the previous evening for a class assignment. I was very impressed by the quality of the PowerPoint and told him so. I had not been aware this was a strength of his and asked how he had become so proficient in using PowerPoint. James was very excited to tell me about developing this skill, and I told him that made me very happy, especially because I knew that he'd had a hard afternoon the day before. I told him that sometimes mistakes get us to where we want to be. James looked at me and said, "I see that from yesterday."

I felt that the first interaction between James and I helped set the stage for him to complete the PowerPoint later that evening and share it with me the following day. James had thought of himself as a failure after his mistake because he did not live up to his expectations. My comments to him were to help normalize making mistakes and encourage James to see them as opportunities to learn. He was able to go home and create an excellent PowerPoint later that day, which demonstrated that he understood this. It allowed him to take a risk without the frustration with what had happened previously carrying over to the evening. Showing me his creation demonstrated that he felt accepted by me and proud of himself.

Gratitude In the Classroom

Charles Dickens, author of the beloved classic, *A Christmas Story*, underscored the importance of gratitude in our lives with this quote about blessings and misfortunes.

> Reflect upon your present blessings, of which every man has plenty; not on your past misfortunes, of which all men have some.[24]

Gratitude is an emotion teachers can help their students understand and appreciate. According to Robert Emmons, a foremost authority on the topic, gratitude has two stages. In the first stage, there is an acknowledgment that goodness is in our lives. We feel that "life is good and has elements worth living." The second phase of gratitude is "recognizing the sources of this gratitude lie, at least partially, outside of ourselves."[25] Thus, the object for gratitude can be external, whether a person, animal, or spiritual force. This makes gratitude different from any other emotion. While you can be angry, happy, ashamed, or proud of yourself internally, we direct our thanks outward. Being grateful confirms that we feel there is some good in the world. Gratitude is a gateway to connection, motivation, discipline, and growth.

Practicing gratitude has a host of benefits. Research confirms that an attitude of gratitude promotes positive emotional health; specifically lower rates of depression while promoting more powerful feelings of joy, optimism, and tranquility. Medically, those who practice gratitude have more robust immune systems and reduced rates of stress-related illnesses. The practice of gratitude increases dopamine, a powerful neurotransmitter that promotes positive feelings within our brain.[26]

Given the benefits of recognizing and acknowledging the positive things in life and the impact expressing gratitude can have, how can teachers work to cultivate this powerful emotion within our students? A variety of research-based exercises can do just that. A few strategies follow.

Three Good Things

In this exercise, students are asked to write down three things that went well for them that particular day. It does not matter if they are big or small things. Ask the students to explain how they contributed to the occurrence of these positive events. So, for example, if a student writes that they are very grateful for their strong performance on an exam, the allowance they received that day, or the praise from a teacher in class, inquire about what they did to make that happen. Focusing on good things that happen to us cultivates gratitude and enhances our overall well-being. This exercise also helps to train the mind to scan for positives. For example, if a student notes that they received a good grade on a test, you might ask how they contributed to that result: You didn't get that good grade by accident – did you study? Did you try to pay more attention in class? Did you ask for help? This helps children see the role they have in making good things happen.

Gratitude Letter

Ask your students to write a letter to someone to express appreciation or thanks. In one study, students who wrote gratitude letters showed increased positive emotions immediately after writing and delivering the letter to the intended recipient, with this state lasting more than two months.[27] Consider a school-wide assembly in which students have the opportunity to share their letters with the recipient in person as a surprise.

Encourage students to express gratitude, perhaps by writing a letter to a veteran thanking them for their service. Practice expressing gratitude or thanks for things that go well in class to model this behavior. Assign books or stories about gratitude. Enhancing gratitude in students can be fun and, in the process, a meaningful lifelong lesson.

Gratitude Journals

Students who kept daily gratitude journals for a short time were more satisfied with their school – even three weeks afterward – than students who did not journal. Students who journaled about things they were grateful for also felt fewer negative emotions, experienced greater satisfaction with their home life, and were more optimistic.[28] In contrast to the *Three Good Things* exercise, the student can list as many things as come to mind in their journal.

Gratitude Scavenger Hunt

Have your students go on a gratitude scavenger hunt either in school or at home and share those items that tap into this emotion with the class. For instance, students can bring in various items that illustrate their favorite color, make them happy or laugh, taste good, enjoy doing, make them proud of themselves, or help them accomplish a goal; they can also create something. Other items can be added, and after presenting the items to the class, a discussion can be held about why they feel thankful for their choices.

Gratitude Jar

Other strategies include bringing a jar to class and asking students to write down things they are grateful for on paper along with their names and put them in the jar. Every few weeks, read the notes aloud in class and ask the child why they felt grateful; this will reinforce the feeling of thankfulness. Alternatively, if the items on the slips of paper seem to be very personal, rather than identify the student who put the slip of paper in the jar, the teacher could just open the discussion by relating to it and asking if any other student could relate to it also.

Gratitude Flower

Younger students can make gratitude flowers by either cutting out a flower template and putting their names in the center while drawing something they are grateful for on each petal or dictating to the teacher who can write these on the petals. The petals can be glued to the center of the flower, which is then placed on a wall to "grow" a gratitude garden for the entire class to see. Alternatively, have the class go through the ABCs and name something they are grateful for that begins with each letter. I know of one instance in which a child came home from school with a turkey made of construction paper by tracing their hands and fingers, but each of the "finger feathers" had one thing the boy was thankful for in his life – Mama, Nannie, cats, pumpkin pie, Elmo time on TV. His mother made similar turkeys that night and shared them with the rest of the family at Thanksgiving dinner. It made him proud!

A curriculum was developed by Dr. Jeffrey J. Froh and his associates [29,30] to promote grateful thinking in elementary school children. In addition, the Greater Good Science Center at the University of California at Berkley offers free online resources for teachers providing a curriculum that fosters awareness and recognition of gratitude.[31]

Neuroplasticity

Nobel prize winning neuroscientist and pathologist, Santiago Ramón y Cajal, describes the ability of the brain to adapt in an intriguing and imaginative way.

> Any man could, if he were so inclined, be the sculptor of his own brain.[32]

Is anatomy indeed destiny? It was previously believed that the human organism was limited by its genetic endowment and had a ceiling on what it could accomplish. For example, Roger Bannister was a distance runner in Great Britain in the 1950s. At that time, the record for running a mile was 4.01 minutes, and scientists said it was a biological given that no human being could run it in less than four minutes. Not only was it impossible, but it was thought to be dangerous. However, despite this well-established scientific "certainty," on May 6, 1954, Bannister broke the record for running a mile in under four minutes, performing the feat with a time of 3:59.4. This was hailed as an incredible achievement. Since then, nearly 1500 people have broken the four-minute mile mark. What was once considered a biological given was proven wrong as the previously accepted limit was repeatedly shattered.

The idea that limits can indeed be broken is an exciting concept for teachers and students. This notion of challenging biological imperatives has gained significant traction and has been researched extensively. Neuroplasticity is the ability of the brain to adapt to changes in an individual's environment by forming new neural connections over time. It explains how the human brain can adapt, master new skills, store memories and information, and even recover after a traumatic brain injury. This is a change from earlier-held beliefs that the brain is hardwired and intractable after childhood.

Celeste Campbell has further explained neuroplasticity in the following way:

> It refers to the physiological changes in the brain that happen as the result of our interactions with our environment. From the time the brain begins to develop in utero until the day we die, the connections among the cells in our brains reorganize in response to our changing needs. This dynamic process allows us to learn from and adapt to different experiences.[33]

Anatomy is not destiny after all.

Exciting new research confirms that this phenomenon is apparent in ways never previously thought. In one instance, the brains of Buddhist monks who engaged in several hours of daily meditation were compared to those who had only recently become monks. Those monks who had been meditating for years had more fully developed regions of their brain associated with empathy than those of the newcomers. Meditation had increased the size of the frontal lobes for those monks who had regularly practiced it compared to those who had not. Consistent meditators had a more significant number of alpha waves associated with less tension, negative mood, sadness, and anger.[34]

There is also the case of long-time London taxi drivers who must pass a test assessing their knowledge of the city's layout – with more than 60,000 streets – without using a map. When the brains of these drivers were scanned, it was found that the hippocampus, the part of the brain associated with spatial reasoning, was more significantly developed than non-taxi drivers. Years of driving around London had imprinted the city's layout onto their brains![35]

Neuroplasticity also has significant implications for those who suffer a stroke or traumatic brain injury. A damaged brain can recover by repairing itself with repeated training and instruction. This impacts how rehabilitation efforts can be structured to help restore brain function.

While these findings are fascinating in medical science, it is tantalizing to consider this phenomenon in a classroom setting. Can teachers impact the development and growth of the brain through their interactions with students? It would appear that this is indeed the case.

Neuroscientists have established that learning changes the brain. Teachers can play a pivotal role in facilitating this process. When students were informed that they could change their brains by learning, significant effects on their overall morale and grades were evident. This knowledge gave students the belief that they could strengthen their brains if they worked hard, just as physical exercise builds muscle. When students adopted this idea, they did better academically than a control group that was not introduced to the concept of neuroplasticity.[36] The notion that students can direct their brains to grow and become stronger is powerful and gives students a sense of control over their growth.

In the classroom, teachers can incorporate an understanding of neuroplasticity in various ways. Encouraging students to repeat activities, retrieve memories, and review the material in various ways leads to thicker, stronger, and higher numbers of connections in the brain. By avoiding rote memorization and placing newly learned material in the context of familiar concepts, the learning process becomes easier as the material can be more readily assimilated. Teaching students study skills is an essential first step in helping children see they can have tools at their disposal to assist them in learning, retaining, synthesizing, and applying substantive material.

Communicating to students that academic growth is not preordained but that their brains can be changed via studying can also enhance motivation; their mindset can shift from "I am not smart" to "I can grow my brain." Teaching this concept to children can give them a powerful tool to fight against hopelessness and despair, giving them a degree of control over their lives and the ability to author their own stories and eventually discover their untapped potential.

In addition to facilitating brain development through academics, human connection is another variable that can promote the same outcome. In his outstanding book, *Social: Why Our Brains Are Wired to Connect*, psychologist and neuroscientist Matthew Lieberman presents cutting-edge research on the way relationships produce physiological changes in the brain.[37] For instance, human brains are the largest of any mammal. Scientists think this is related to the ability of humans to socialize in a manner beyond other species. Socializing activates the pleasure centers of the brain. A strong, mutually satisfying relationship between teacher and student can positively impact both brains.

When students feel that their teachers care about them, brain responses can facilitate learning and motivation. Connections both interpersonally and neurologically are strengthened when a teacher implicitly and explicitly communicates to the student how happy they are to be their teacher.

Flow

Kobe Bryant All-Star pro basketball player knew about going with the flow.

> It's hard to describe. You just feel so confident. You get your feet set and get a good look at the basket – it's going in. Even the ones I missed I thought were going in …. I never thought I would have a game like this, though. I made the first one. I said, "Let me see if I can make two." I made the second one; I said, "Let me see if I can make three." I made the third one, I said, "I've got a rhythm going."[38]
>
> Kobe Bryant, All-Star NBA Player

On January 7, 2003, the late Kobe Bryant, an all-star basketball player for the Los Angeles Lakers, set an NBA scoring record by sinking twelve three-point shots, including nine in a row, in a single game. This was an incredible achievement, and since that game, just two other players have tied him; only three have surpassed him.

Bryant's explanation of having a "rhythm" speaks to feeling locked in or on automatic pilot. He felt that things were working, and there was no reason to believe that they would stop working in the same way. This experience in producing consistent results is a phenomenon that is not all that unusual. Athletes refer to this feeling by describing themselves as "being on fire" or "being in the zone." It is a feeling of extreme confidence that you will succeed, that nothing can stop you as you are "in the groove." In writing about this, author John Passaro explains.

When the zone calls, you must listen. You never know how long being in the zone lasts. It is a cardinal rule – you must take advantage of every second that you are in the zone.[39]

This feeling of being in the zone is not limited to athletes. Musicians, comedians, and other performers experience a situation when they are razor-sharp in their performance, hitting levels previously not obtained. While sustained practice plays a crucial role in making this happen, it is hard to describe how the experience occurs. In writing about how musicians experience this phenomenon, writer Jane Horvath, a musician herself, attempts to put this almost transcendent event into words.

You can hardly believe it when you experience that rare, perfect moment when your gestures, feelings, senses, and your mind are in perfect harmony. When everything "gels," you sound like you do in your mind – like Heifetz, Rubinstein, James Galway, or Alison Balsom! You've had an out-of-body experience, and your elation at the simplicity, focus, and depth renders you whole, complete, and joyful. Athletes speak of searching to recreate that feeling of being "in the zone" – entirely concentrated and focused yet at ease with what they are doing. It's a high in itself!

Similarly, when we musicians meld perfectly into oneness with our instrument, body and mind, music and the creative process can be experienced viscerally. The freedom to express the music comes so naturally that everyone – you *and your listeners feel the flow.*[40]

Emphasis added

Hovarth's use of the word "flow" is quite apt.

How optimal experiences impact people and use flow has been described by psychologist Mihally Csikszentmihalyi.

Imagine being able to foster this state in your students. Their motivation would be at an all-time high, and their effort would be smooth and consistent. While their engagement in the task presented to them would be substantial, students engaged in the state of flow are excited about learning for its own sake and strive to reach their potential.[41]

Teachers can encourage the development of flow in the classroom by modifying their lessons in specific ways, for instance, by choosing material that challenges students without being overly complicated. If it is too challenging, students may feel stressed; if it is too easy, they may find it boring. In either case, the student may give up. Teachers need to present material in that sweet spot, where it is not so easy as to be boring nor so challenging as to be intimidating. Teachers want to challenge students while holding their interest. Further, helping students understand the relevancy of concepts to their lives will promote greater interest in the material, a fundamental condition of flow, as demonstrated by the earlier example of helping a student relate physics to basketball.

While these and other pedagogical methods help foster and maintain a state of flow in students, our focus is primarily on the teacher-student relationship. Can this variable influence a student's ability to enter a state of flow? Some preliminary research indicates that it may indeed be the case. The relationship you have with your student, in conjunction with various teaching strategies can be a helpful ally in achieving it.[42]

David Shernoff, an educational researcher, has studied flow in the classroom and discovered a connection between states of flow and positive teacher-student relationships.[43] Teachers who prioritize building a relationship with their students hasten the development of flow in the classroom by promoting a desire to engage with the material, a necessary condition for flow to develop. Shernoff also posits the notion that humor in lessons can increase flow. Not only does this help maintain student interest, but also models a high level of enthusiasm for a subject. This can shift a classroom lesson from a dull experience to a high-interest activity. Combining a positive teacher-student relationship and presenting engaging, age-appropriate material at a student's skill level will promote greater student engagement and enhanced motivation, setting the stage for flow.

The experience of teachers finding themselves in a flow state while presenting their lessons is also a genuine phenomenon. Research indicates that the enthusiasm of teachers who experience a flow state while presenting a lesson can be contagious to their students.[44] In a sense, the teacher-student relationship can function as a closed loop with the participants' attitudes and behaviors reverberating between (some would describe as "bouncing off") each other. When asked to identify the causes of their own flow experiences, teachers reported that their students' level of engagement contributed significantly. When in the flow state, teachers report feeling connected to their class and sensed the class's heightened attentiveness.[45]

Emotional Intelligence

Dale Carnegie gained popularity and renown for the development of self-improvement methods, the forerunner of positive thinking strategies:

> When dealing with people, remember you are not dealing with creatures of logic but with creatures of emotion.[46]

A student's intellectual capacity is undoubtedly an essential consideration in helping them succeed. However, Dr. Daniel Goleman[47] and other investigators such as Drs. John Mayer, Robert Sternberg, and Peter Salovey[48] have developed an understanding of what would be called "emotional intelligence" or E.I. Until their concept was introduced in the mid-1990s, the primacy of I.Q. or the intelligence quotient had been a given since it had been widely adopted at the beginning of the 20th century. However, as seen in Goleman's work, humans have an entirely different and additional skill set to enhance their functioning. Emotional Intelligence is the ability to understand, use, and manage your own emotions in positive ways to relieve stress, communicate effectively, empathize with others, overcome challenges, and defuse conflict.

Emotional Intelligence is comprised of the following abilities:

♦ accurately perceive, appraise and express emotion;
♦ accessing or generating feelings on demand when they can facilitate understanding of self or others;
♦ understanding emotions and the knowledge that derives from them; and
♦ regulating emotions to promote emotional and intellectual growth.

These areas have a significant impact on a student's ability to succeed academically and flourish socially. Awareness of these can be an essential part of the teacher-student relationship.

This notion of humans having non-cognitive skills that impact behavior and emotions has gained widespread acceptance. Even in the world of technology, which places a premium on computer skills, analytics, and math skills, a potential employer will also assess E.I. skills by holding nontechnical behavioral interviews with potential employees to assess their ability to relate to others, handle adversity adaptively, and predict whether other employees and management would be able to work with them easily.

Research demonstrates a strong connection between student capacity for emotional intelligence and academic success.

The higher a student's emotional quotient, the higher the level of academic achievement.[49] E.I. helps students by coping adaptively with academic stressors such as assessment and group collaboration. In fact, after intelligence and conscientiousness, E.I. was the third significant indicator predictive of student success. One of the benefits of having a higher level of E.I. can be seen in student performance in the humanities.[50] Self-rated scales of E.I. given to students were more effective predictors of academic success than standardized achievement tests or student grades.[51] As Carol McCann, a psychologist who has studied the relationship between E.I. and academic achievement, stated, "It's not enough to be smart and hardworking. Students must also be able to understand and manage their emotions to succeed at school."[52]

Dr. McCann and her colleagues reviewed over 160 studies from more than 25 countries that included over 40,000 students at all age levels from elementary through college. The results consistently showed that higher E.I. was associated with higher grades and test scores regardless of age. McCann notes that students with higher levels of E.I. can better regulate their emotions, keeping negative emotions in check. These students are motivated to maintain positive social relationships with teachers, peers, and their families, thus predisposing them to greater academic success.[53]

Teachers should not have to choose between facilitating students' growth on either the scholastic or emotional front. It is not an either/or proposition. Being attentive to a student's psychological life will come naturally, especially when your relationship with them is rooted in a positive strength-based perspective. This can be accomplished by teachers keeping the following points in mind:

◆ be aware of your student's emotions;
◆ see emotions as an opportunity for connecting and teaching;
◆ listen and validate student feelings;
◆ help students label their emotions;
◆ help students problem-solve within limits.

There are many methods to help students become more emotionally intelligent beings. While there are formal curricula school districts can purchase that feature emotional intelligence lessons, I will focus instead on how teachers can seamlessly weave E.I. concepts into interactions with their students.

Modeling and highlighting positive emotions and behavior for students in your interactions with them and during lessons is a great place to start. Teaching students the importance of having good values, being honest, trustworthy, and taking responsibility for one's actions can be incorporated into academic content such as history and literature lessons. Doing this provides real-life validity of their value.

If a student is having a hard day, talk to them about how they feel and how this is connected to how they are behaving. Communicate to them that emotion is valued in your classroom. You can have concrete lessons on different aspects of emotions for young students to help them recognize different feelings in themselves and peers.

In reading and literature, teachers can ask in class discussions or on assessments how a character in a book or play might be feeling at any given point in the story. Students can then relate to how they might feel under similar circumstances, then predict how the character will react next. Tie feelings to behavior and ask if the character's behavior is realistic under the circumstances. In higher grades, this can be incorporated into an area such as history. For instance: How might President Truman have felt about his decision to bomb Hiroshima, Japan to end World War II? This can trigger a discussion on feelings.

Additional practices that can be used in the classroom to enhance a student's understanding of managing feelings can also include:

◆ Showing students pictures of faces and asking them to identify the emotion depicted. After your student identifies the feeling, have them mimic the face using a mirror to get immediate feedback to reinforce this further.
◆ Asking students to notice the posture of others as well as their own. How a person manages their body can

often reveal more information than the words they are using. Using photographs, drawings, or still-frames from a movie, ask students to describe a person's posture. Students can be asked to model how people feel in certain situations, such as winning the lottery or watching their favorite football team lose a close game.

◆ Asking young students to identify the emotions in others to show their degree of understanding. For instance, students can pick cards with emotions on them and play "feelings charades" and guess the feeling depicted in the game.

◆ Recognizing tone of voice is another cue to a person's emotional state, much like body language. Students can practice what it sounds like to be happy, sad, angry, or other emotions while showing them how it sounds not to have those emotions despite feeling them. This can assist students in recognizing the voice as an emotional cue.

◆ Encouraging students to listen for understanding, not merely to respond. This would allow students to tune into some of the points we have considered, such as facial expression, tone of voice, eye contact, and posture. This can help a student understand what a peer or adult – even the teacher – is trying to express.

◆ Helping students become more attuned and comfortable identifying their feelings and those of others can assist them in becoming kinder and more empathic.

This inclusive view of emotions can go a long way toward helping students grow academically and interpersonally while experiencing fewer behavioral difficulties. In addition, it will allow them to enjoy school and attend more regularly, helping them to tune in and participate in class and come to school better prepared. Other than parents or close family members, you are among the primary adults in your student's lives, regardless of age, that can model and convey how important it is to understand and acknowledge their emotions.

A teacher who values the role of E.I. in the classroom is open to refining these skills in themselves. You need to be kind to yourself and set aside some time to meet your own emotional needs. Devoting time to hobbies, meditating, spending time in nature, or just allowing yourself to binge-watch a favorite TV show can allow you to de-stress and be more emotionally available to your students, as well as your family and friends. Providing self-care will enable you to meet your student's needs more effectively while teaching them how to manage the world of feelings.

Applying the Strength-Based Model to Students with Disabilities

Shane E Bryan who suffered from dystonia, a painful and debilitating neuromuscular disease understood that disability is a two-sided coin.

> I do not have a disability; I have a gift! Others may see it as a disability, but I see it as a challenge. This challenge is a gift because I have to become stronger to get around it, and smarter to figure out how to use it; others should be so lucky.[54]

There are countless examples of people overcoming adversity to achieve their goals – here are a few. Jessica Long was born in Siberia and raised in an orphanage. She was diagnosed with fibular hemimelia, a condition in which the fibulas, ankles, heels, and most of the other bones in the feet are missing. Jessica, however, became a Paralympic swimmer and won over 20 medals. Erik Weihenmeyer lost his vision at age 14 yet successfully climbed Mt. Everest. Surfer Bethany Hamilton was back on her surfboard less than a month after losing her arm in a shark attack – two years later, she was a national surfing champion.

These stories of triumph over the odds are inspiring. Most importantly, these remarkable people did not give up on themselves. They refused to accept "I can't."

The good news is that a student does not have to experience challenges of the magnitude these incredible athletes have to reap the benefits of a strength-based approach. I regularly quote countless others who demonstrate perseverance, tenacity, and grit. Whether you are a teacher, life coach, or therapist, helping children understand the value of these lessons can be life-changing, especially if the student has constraints that profoundly impact their lives.

As psychologist Robert Brooks so aptly writes, we all have "islands of competence" or signature strengths.[55] Unfortunately, teachers may not have the time to look at a child holistically to see past their struggles. A strength-based teacher orients students toward digging, if necessary, to locate the buried treasure within.

When working with disabled students, using a strength-based model does not mean minimizing or using semantics to sugarcoat their difficulties. Instead, it keeps the primary focus on finding their strengths and on growth.

A strength-based approach is implemented by Florida special education teacher Christopher Ulmer who begins his school day by complimenting his students.[56] Ulmer has posted videos on social media (with parental permission) and the response has been tremendous. He conveys hope to students by focusing on what is right about them instead of their shortcomings. Ulmer reports that his special education students, including those classified as autistic, having a traumatic brain injury, or speech apraxia, look forward to this morning ritual of compliments, and the effects have been significant.[57] Ulmer reports that not only do his students enjoy receiving compliments but also their overall social adjustment has improved. For instance, these students have shown confidence in participating in various extracurricular activities, which many would have thought impossible to achieve.

The psychiatrist and international authority on ADHD quoted earlier, Edward Hallowell, offers a framework to view its symptoms as potential assets instead of problematic behaviors (see Table 4.1).[58] Presenting this view to an individual diagnosed with ADHD immediately provides hope and optimism to counteract hopelessness and fear. In the chart below, Hallowell presents the symptoms of ADHD in a positive strength-based way. Conveying this mindset to a child can be liberating for them.

I have used this framework with parents and children, and the shift in their perceptions has been palpable. Viewing a

TABLE 4.1 Reframing Of ADHD Symptoms In a Strength-Based Model

Negative Trait of ADD	Positive Trait of ADD
Hyperactive, restless	Energetic
Intrusive	Eager
Can't stay on point	Sees connections others don't
Forgetful	Gets totally into what s/he is doing
Disorganized	Spontaneous
Stubborn	Persistent, won't give up
Inconsistent	Shows flashes of brilliance
Moody	Sensitive
Impulsive	Creative

behavioral trait not as a negative symptom that weighs the student down but rather as a positive quality can have value and provide hope for their future.

Rebecca Branstetter, a school psychologist, expanded upon this idea.[59] Branstetter cites an instance in which she tested a child who presented as having a learning disability. She explained the assessment results to the child using a model of the brain. Branstetter told the child that they had particular strengths and needed to do " 'brain pushups' to get stronger." This was incredibly reassuring to the child, who now not only understood why they had difficulty reading but, in a very familiar term she could relate to, understood this was something that could be managed. Branstetter explains to a child that a label can help everyone understand why they are struggling in a particular area to receive help.

In my 30 years as a school psychologist, the opportunity to apply strength-based principles in working with students with challenges was one of the highlights of my job. The opportunity to watch students experience success when it had eluded them was incredibly gratifying for me, as well as the student.

Strength-Based Individual Education Plan (IEPs)

An experienced classroom teacher, Laura Lenz, understands the importance and value in identifying a student's strengths.

When you point out kids' strengths, they grow in confidence. They know you see them. You see the whole individual, not just an empty vessel that needs to be filled with your knowledge.[60]

As a school psychologist, one of my duties included preparing Individual Education Plans (IEPs) for special education classes. These documents review the needs and goals of the student and serve as a blueprint for the teacher or special education service provider to follow. They focus primarily on student deficits and often do not do enough to highlight their strengths. The notion of creating strength-based IEPs to emphasize student assets has many merits. Working from a document that highlights strengths can change a teacher's mindset and approach from repairing deficits to growing strengths that can powerfully influence their interactions with students. Understanding student strengths can foster a more personal connection between a teacher and a student, which can help enhance the motivation of both. Such a document does not offer a cursory look at assets but rather a framework that weaves this information into its goals. This helps students understand and believe they can strengthen their abilities and encourages them to make appropriate choices to attain those goals.

A strength-based IEP does not mean areas of weakness are ignored; it encompasses challenging areas as well as students' assets. However, enhanced awareness of what students can do will increase the likelihood of incorporating this knowledge to create goals and help the student achieve them. An IEP can create a more focused, direct approach to learning in the long run. When appropriate, include the student to help identify their strengths, preferences, and interests. An IEP is a roadmap for school staff and faculty to follow, and by paying greater attention to strengths, it can take teachers and students along the most fulfilling route to get to the destination. It can significantly impact the mindset of students, teachers, and even school psychologists!

Utilizing a strength-based approach in the classroom is in harmony with a positive teacher-student relationship. Presenting opportunities to help children discover their hidden treasures will help them unlock their potential and strengthen their bond with you. This chapter has shown how to utilize various modalities to apply the tenets of a strength-based philosophy to working with students.

Fostering a growth mindset and intrinsic motivation, normalizing and removing the stigma of making mistakes, and promoting gratitude practices in your classroom will enhance the learning process. It will also help transform your relationship with students to motivate them to do their best. Introducing students to the idea of neuroplasticity, fostering flow, and developing emotional intelligence combine to make stronger students. Being able to conceptualize academic and behavioral challenges and reframe them in a strength-based model is a precious gift to offer your students.

References

1. Sparks, S. (2019). "Why teacher-student relationships matter." *Education Week*. Website. www.edweek.org/teaching-learning/why-teacher-student-relationships-matter/2019/03
2. Maraboli, S. www.goodreads.com/quotes/tag/mindset
3. Paquette, J. (2015). *Real Happiness: Proven Paths for Contentment, Peace & Well Being*. Pesi Publishing & Media.
4. Bronson, P. (2007, Feb. 19). "How not to talk to your kids: The Inverse Power of praise." *New York Magazine*.
5. Economy, P. (2015, November 5). *Inc.* www.inc.com/peter-economy/26-brilliant-quotes-on-the-super-power-of-words.html
6. Bass, S. *Saul Bass Quotes*. www.goodreads.com/quotes/tag/intrinsic-motivation
7. Ryan, R. & Deci, E. (2017). *Self-Determination Theory: Basic Psychological Needs in Motivation, Development, and Wellness*. Guilford Press.
8. Ibid.
9. Ibid.
10. Ibid.
11. Ibid.

12. Ibid.

13. Daum, K. (2016, February 11). "37 quotes from Thomas Edison that will inspire success." *Inc.* www.inc.com/kevin-daum/37-quotes-from-thomas-edison-that-will-bring-out-your-best.html

14. Michou, A., Vansteenkiste,M., Mouratidis, A., &. Lens, W. (2014). "Enriching the hierarchical model of achievement motivation: Autonomous and controlling reasons underlying achievement goals." *British Journal of Educational Psychology*, 84, 650–666.

15. Boaler, J. (2019). *Limitless Mind: Learn, Lead, and Live Without Barriers*. Harper One.

16. Tereda, Y. (2020, November 19). "The mistake imperative – Why we must get over our fear of student error." *Edutopia*. www.edutopia.org/article/mistake-imperative-why-we-must-get-over-our-fear-student-error

17. Schleppenbach, M., Flevares, L., Sims, L., & Perry, M. (2007). "Teachers' responses to student mistakes in Chinese and U.S. mathematics classrooms." *The Elementary School Journal*, 108(2), 131–147.

18. Leonard, J., Lee, Y., & Schulz, L. (2017, September 22). "Infants make more attempts to achieve a goal when they see adults persist." *Science*, 357(6357), 1290–1294.

19. Johnson J., Panagioti, M., Bass, J., Ramsey, L., & Harrison, R. (2017, March). "Resilience to emotional distress in response to failure, error or mistakes: A systematic review." *Clinical Psychology Review*, 52, 19–42.

20. Piper, W. (2020). *The Little Engine That Could*. Grosset & Dunlap.

21. Santat, D. (2017). *After The Fall (How Humpty Dumpty Got Back Up Again)*. Roaring Book Press.

22. Beaty, B. (2013). *Rosie Revere, Engineer*. Harry N. Abrams.

23. Muder, C. *Forbes Field Couldn't Contain Willie Stargell*. National Baseball Hall of Fame. https://baseballhall.org/discover/inside-pitch/forbes-field-couldnt-contain-stargell

24. www.goodreads.com/quotes/21915-reflect-upon-your-present-blessings----of-which-every-man

25. Emmons, R. (2008). *Thanks! How Practicing Gratitude Can Make You Happier*. Houghton Mifflin.

26. Ibid.

27. Eva, A. (2018) *Three Ways to Cultivate Gratitude at School*. The Greater Good Science Center. https://greatergood.berkeley.edu/article/item/three_ways_to_cultivate_gratitude_at_school

28. Ibid.

29. Froh, J. & Bono, G. (2012) *How to Foster Gratitude In Schools*. The Greater Good Science Center. https://greatergood.berkeley.edu/article/item/how_to_foster_gratitude_in_schools

30. Froh, J., Bono, G., Fan, J., Emmons, R., Henderson, K., Harris, C., Leggio, H., & Wood, A. (2014, June) "Nice thinking! An educational intervention that teaches children to think gratefully." *School Psychology Review*, 43(2), 132–151.

31. Greater Good Science Center. (2022). Gratitude Curricula https://ggsc.berkeley.edu/who_we_serve/educators/educator_resources/gratitude_curricula)

32. www.goodreads.com/quotes/185999-any-man-could-if-he-were-so-inclined-be-the

33. Neurohealth Associates. (2019, April,3). "What is neuroplasticity, and how can i help my brain get stronger?"https://nhahealth.com/what-is-neuroplasticity-and-how-can-i-help-my-brain-get-stronger/#:~:text=Neuroplasticity%20is%20the%20brain's%20amazing,our%20interactions%20with%20our%20environment

34. Gilsinan, K. (2015, July 4). "The Buddhist and the neuroscientist." *The Atlantic*. www.theatlantic.com/health/archive/2015/07/dalai-lama-neuroscience-compassion/397706/

    See also Davidson, R. & Lutz, A. (2008). "Buddha's brain: Neuroplasticity and meditation." IEEE Signal Processing Magazine, 25(1), 176–174. https://doi.org/10.1109/msp.2008.4431873

    See also Goleman, D. & Davidson, R. (2018, May 7). "How meditation changes your brain – and your life." www.lionsroar.com/how-meditation-changes-your-brain-and-your-life/

35. Jabr, F. (2011, December 8). "Cache cab: Taxi drivers' brains grow to navigate London's streets." *Scientific American*. www.scientificamerican.com/article/london-taxi-memory

36. Su, Y., Veeravagu A., & Grant, G. (2016) "Neuroplasticity after traumatic brain injury." In Laskowitz, D. & Grant, G., eds. *Translational Research in Traumatic Brain Injury*. CRC Press/Taylor and Francis Group, pp. 163–179.

37. Leiberman, M. (2014). *Social: Why Our Brains Are Wired to Connect*. Crown.
38. Huges, G. (2014, February 3) "The zone, according to past and present superstars." https://bleacherreport.com/articles/1946021-the-zone-according-to-nba-superstars-past-and-present
39. Passaro, J. (2013). "In the zone and other sports essays." Createspace.
40. Hovarth, J. (2015, February, 28)). "In the zone – How performers do it." https://interlude.hk/zone-performers/
41. Csikezentmihalyi, M. (1990). *Flow: The Psychology of Optimal Experience*. Harper Collins.
42. Ibid.
43. Shernoff, D., Abdi, B., Anderson, B. & Czikezentmihalyi, M. (2014). "Flow in schools revisited: Cultivating engaged learners and optimal learning environments." In Furlong, M., Gilman, R., & Heubner, S. (2014). *Handbook Of Positive Psychology in The Schools*, Routledge, pp. 211–226.
44. Bakker, A. (2005). "Flow among music teachers and their students: The crossover of peak experiences." *Journal of Vocational Behavior*, 66, 26 – 44.
45. Basom, M. & Frase, L. (2004). "Creating optimal work environments: Exploring teacher flow experiences." *Mentoring and Tutoring*, 12, 241–258.
46. Tregold, G. (2016, August 4). "55 inspiring quotes that show the power of emotional intelligence." www.inc.com/gordon-tredgold/55-inspiring-quotes-that-show-the-importance-of-emotional-intelligence.html
47. Goleman, D. (2005). *Emotional Intelligence*, 10th ed. Bantam.
48. Rackett, M., Delaney, S., & Salovey, P. (2021). "Emotional intelligence." In R. Biswas-Diener & E. Diener (eds.), *Psychology*. (Noba textbook series). DEF publishers. http://noba.to/xzvpfun7
49. Bodine, R. & Crawford, D. (1999). *Developing Intelligence. A Guide to Behavior Management and Conflict Resolution in Schools*. McNaughton & Gunn.
    See also Suleman, Q., Hussain, I., Syed, M., Parveen R., Lodhi, I. & Mahmood, Z. (2019) "Association between emotional intelligence and academic success among undergraduates: A cross-sectional study in Kust." Pakistan. PLoS ONE 14(7): e0219468. https://doi.org/10.1371/journal.pone.0219468

See also Saeed, W. & Ahmad, R. (2020, March) "Association of demographic characteristics, emotional intelligence and academic self-efficacy among undergraduate students." *Journal of Pakistan Medical Association*, 70(3), 457–460. doi: 10.5455/JPMA.11384. PMID: 32207425.

See also *International Journal of Managerial Studies and Research (IJMSR)*. (2019) 3(9).

See also *Psychological Bulletin American Psychological Association* (2020, September 15)). 146(2), 150–186,

50. MacCann, C., Jiang, Y., & Brown, L. (2020). "Emotional intelligence predicts academic performance: A meta-analysis psychological bulletin." *American Psychological Association*, 146(2), 150–186. http://dx.doi.org/10.1037/

51. Ibid.

52. Ibid.

53. Ibid.

54. Vantage Mobility International. "30 incredibly inspiring quotes for people with disabilities." www.vantagemobility.com/blog/incredi bly-inspiring-quotes-for-people-with-disabilities

55. Brooks, B. & Goldstein, S. (2002). *Raising Resilient Children: Fostering Strength, Hope And Optimism In Your Child*. McGraw Hill.

56. Brown, G. (2015, November 17)). "Florida Teacher Starts Each Day Complimenting Students One by One." https://abcnews.go.com/Lifestyle/florida-teacher-starts-day-complimenting-students/story?id=35259600

57. Ibid.

58. Hallowell, E. "ADHD Across the Life Span." Workshop attended August 2016 at Cape Cod Institute, Eastham, MA.

59. Branstetter, R. (2019, September, 10)). "How to help students with learning disabilities focus on their strengths." *Greater Good Magazine*. https://greatergood.berkeley.edu/article/item/how_to_help_students_with_learning_disabilities_focus_on_their_st rengths

60. Lenz, L. (2016, September, 11). "A Strength-Based Approach To Teaching English As Second Language." www.cultofpedagogy.com/strength-based-teaching-esl/

5

Additional Strength-Based Interventions for the Classroom

Ned Hallowell, who had a difficult time in school in part because of undiagnosed Attention Deficit Disorder (ADD), benefited from the connection his teachers made with him. He eventually became a psychiatrist and expert on ADD

> They didn't know how much they were helping me just by being there, just by connecting with me in an ordinary teacher-like way.[1]
>
> Ned Hallowell, Psychiatrist

This chapter will draw from positive psychology and allied fields to identify additional strength-based interventions that can be incorporated into the classroom to enhance your relationship with your students. The beauty of thinking within a strength-based framework is that the teacher is encouraged to use their creativity to tailor interventions to meet student needs. In this model, the teacher does not have to be bound to specific prescriptions for success but can feel free to improvise.

DOI: 10.4324/9781003368014-6

Mindfulness to Reduce Student Stress

While the roots of mindfulness date back over two thousand years, it has more recently become a mainstreamed method to reduce stress by becoming more aware of the present. This is described by Jon-Kabat-Zinn, a proponent of the practice of mindfulness:

> Mindfulness is a way of befriending ourselves and our experience.[2]

Mindfulness is a mental state achieved by focusing awareness on the present moment while calmly acknowledging and accepting one's feelings, thoughts, and bodily sensations. While mindfulness is often used as a therapeutic intervention to reduce stress in a clinical setting, it also lends itself to use in the classroom.

The David Lynch Foundation for Consciousness-Based Education and World Peace was started by the renowned filmmaker, musician, and writer to fulfill his mission "to ensure that every child anywhere in the world who wanted to learn to meditate could do so."[3] Research confirms that children who meditate have improved attendance and decreased suspension rates,[4] experience an increase in test scores and overall GPA,[5] and have a higher likelihood of graduating.[6] Further, students who engage in meditation also demonstrate a lessening of ADHD symptoms and other learning challenges[7] have increases in overall intelligence and creativity,[8] and significant reductions of anxiety, depression, and overall stress levels.[9] Finally, teachers who engage in mindfulness themselves experience reduced burnout and stress.[10]

Students who practice mindfulness can improve their attention span and regulate their emotions more effectively[11,] allowing them to calm down quickly after becoming upset. In addition, self-esteem and body image improves, as does social relatedness.[12,13]

There are various ways to introduce mindfulness to children. Formal programs geared to group lessons are available; however, that is not the only way to teach your students about mindfulness.

In my work with children, I have discovered simple methods that can be used individually or in a group setting. These are also great ways to introduce calm and serenity into your life to improve your emotional well-being.

To introduce this concept to students, you do not even have to use the term mindfulness, as young children may find it confusing. The goal is for students to engage in the exercises and feel their impact. You can begin by saying, "We will learn ways to help us notice our thoughts, emotions, physical well-being, and things around us." You can mention that this can help us feel relaxed and calmer. Your vocabulary can be adjusted depending on your students' age group and unique needs. Good practice will necessitate you receiving approval from your principal, as well as the parents of students prior to implementing these strategies.

Below are some mindfulness techniques I have used successfully with students. These can be easily adapted for use in the classroom; feel free to use them for yourself. Again, before using these, I would apprise parents of what you would like to do and obtain their permission.

Breathing Buddies

The bedrock of mindfulness is learning to control breathing. It is a prerequisite to experiencing the benefits mindfulness offers. If a student, particularly a younger one, has trouble focusing on their breathing, use a technique called "Breathing Buddies" discussed by Daniel Goleman, the psychologist quoted previously discussing emotional intelligence.[14] Give a student a stuffed animal and ask them to lie on their back with the animal on their belly. The student is instructed to focus their attention on the rise and fall of the stuffed animal as they breathe in and out. This exercise is beneficial in helping children become more attentive and helps regulate distressing emotions when necessary. A variant of this is to have a child breathe while watching their breath go in and out. Doing this exercise for two minutes daily can produce a calm state for the student and assist their brain in focusing on one thing at a time.

Children experience mindfulness more readily when they have a sound to focus on – so incorporate ringing a bell, playing a piano chord, or using chimes or a triangle. Creating a sound and asking the students to listen until it fades and is no longer possible to hear helps them focus on a single thing.

Color Breathing

This exercise is a favorite of many children I have treated – and many adults. The student is asked to sit up straight and close their eyes or look down if they prefer. Ask them to keep their body loose and relaxed, then instruct them to breathe in very slowly through their nose, hold their breath and think of a color that helps them feel calm. Once they do so, they can breathe out slowly through their nose while imagining they are breathing out the color. The exercise can be repeated at least five times. When the students complete the exercise, ask what they are feeling.

Rain Breathing

Have your students close their eyes or look downward and inhale slowly through their noses. Ask them to hold their breath briefly, then slowly exhale through their mouth making a "shh" sound like rain falling. Have them do this at least five times and follow up with a conversation about how it felt.

Circle Breathing

Ask the student to close their eyes or look down while sitting up straight, then put their fingertips together to form a sphere. As they breathe in through their nose, they move their fingers apart, much like holding a ball. As they breathe out through their nose, they simultaneously bring their fingers together to the same position they had initially. Have them do this at least five times and talk afterward about their experience. If a student prefers, you can have them hold a balloon between their hands instead of imagining holding a ball.

Rectangle (Box) Breathing

This is a powerful strategy to reduce stress – the U.S. Navy Seals use it in their training to assist them in staying calm and focused before and after going on missions.[15] In adapting the method for students, have them close their eyes or look down while sitting straight. Instruct them to inhale while counting to four, hold their breath for two counts, exhale counting to four, and wait two seconds before repeating the process. During this time, they draw the four sides of a rectangle with their finger in the air (up one side for 4, over for 2, down the other side for 4, and back to the starting point for 2 to complete the rectangle). Do this at least five times.

Stretching

If you have room in your class, you can have your students lie on their back, arms by their sides, placing the back of their hands on the floor palms up, and hold the pose for five deep breaths. After they do this at least five times, ask the students what they notice.

Stretching # 2

Have your students stand straight with their feet hip-distance apart. Instruct them to lift their arms above their heads to form an "X" and hold it for five deep breaths. Ask what they notice.

Stretching # 3

Ask your students to start on their hands and knees, palms flat on the floor. They can then arch their back upward while tucking their chin in their chest as they take a deep breath. They hold the pose for five deep breaths. Ask them to reflect on their breathing or calmness.

Stretching # 4

Ask your students to sit straight with feet together, then lift their arms to their sides so their body makes a "T." Next, have them bend at the waist slowly, then drop their hands down and forward to touch their knees, shins, and toes while holding the pose for five breaths.

A Mindful Minute

This technique can be especially beneficial for teachers, as well as students.[16]

- ◆ First, close your eyes (although you do not have to), put aside anything you are doing, and follow the steps below.
- ◆ Feel your breath move in and out through your nostrils while also filling your chest and lungs, exhaling slowly.
- ◆ Become attuned with your senses – hear the sounds around you, feel the air temperature against your skin, and notice any tastes, smells, or textures.
- ◆ Notice any emotions and thoughts you are experiencing at this moment. Do not try to change them. Just let them be.
- ◆ If your mind drifts, bring it back to the moment.
- ◆ When you are ready, open your eyes and come fully back.

Even doing this for one minute will help you slow down and become more present.

Exercise

It is hard to imagine a time when physical education was not valued. President John Kennedy changed that, introducing the establishment of a physical fitness curriculum in American schools.

> Intelligence and skills can only function at the peak of their capacity when the body is healthy and strong.[17]

I was not exactly a star athlete and did not value physical education as a child. However, had I known then what I have since learned about the value of exercise, I would have reconsidered my stance. As a teacher, incorporating exercise into your classroom activities, in addition to their regular gym classes, is a fun and easy way to help your students utilize their strengths. At the same time, it can enhance the student-teacher relationship. Before the notion of incorporating exercise is dismissed as a waste of time that takes away valuable learning time, I want to cite some research that blows that idea away.

Let's Get Physical

This phrase is a lyric from the well-known song made famous by Olivia Newton-John.[18] However, as we will soon see, this sage advice not only has significant implications for our overall health but also promotes brain development and learning.

Many parents, educators, pediatricians, and scientists have been decrying the lack of time dedicated to exercise and physical activity for children and also note the amount of time children avoid physical exercise. They cite rising rates of obesity and complications such as childhood diabetes arising from lack of activity. Physical health is not the only thing at stake. In addition to strengthening muscles and organs throughout the body, new evidence has come to light demonstrating the ways exercise impacts the brain.

The Center for Disease Control (CDC) strongly recommends physical exercise to maintain physical health and boost overall brain functioning.[19] Such benefits include higher oxygen levels to the brain promoting higher levels of neurotransmitter activity, better quality of sleep, and reduced risk of dementia. Increased neurotransmitters assure the survival of neurons in areas responsible for learning, memory, and higher thinking. One study demonstrated that in brain scans following 20 minutes of either sedentary or exercise activity of children, a higher level of neurotransmitter activity was seen in the brains of the active group.[20]

Among the benefits of exercise, the CDC notes "physical activity can have an impact on cognitive skills and attitudes and academic behavior, all of which are important components of improved academic performance. These include enhanced concentration and attention, as well as improved classroom behavior."[21] The CDC reviewed data as to the value of having classroom-based physical activity, and it found "positive associations between classroom-based physical activity and indicators of cognitive skills and attitudes, academic behavior, and academic achievement; none of the studies found negative associations."[22]

Exercise primes students for academic success through brain development. As will be seen, several studies connect physical activity to lower absenteeism and dropout rates while confirming that physically active students earn higher grades. In addition, those studies find that physically active students become more socially connected than their less active peers. Attention and concentration skills are also enhanced when a student is active.

A correlation exists between academic achievement and physical fitness.[23] Researchers gathered information about the physical fitness of third, fourth, and fifth graders and examined their performance on cognitive tasks. They then administered tasks requiring visual discrimination of objects. The more fit children processed visual information more rapidly and efficiently, making fewer errors than less fit students. Another study found that students who spent 30 minutes walking on a treadmill increased their test scores by ten percent over the school year. This is because regular exercise enlarges the basal ganglia and hippocampus, areas of the brain that regulate memory and focus.[24] Other research in the United Kingdom found that students aged 7, 11, and 14 who had increased physical activity experienced higher academic achievement.[25]

The Naperville, Illinois school district instituted a morning exercise program to determine if it impacted reading skills; the results demonstrated significant academic growth in that area.[26] In Kansas, study results indicated that "on average, students who are physically fit score above standard on Kansas state assessments in reading and math," according to a press release. The study had more good news to report: physically active kids also miss fewer school days!

While the academic benefits of exercise have been noted, it is essential to point out the considerable social and emotional benefits of physical activity. Exercise has considerably lessened stress, depression, anxiety, and ADHD among students.[27,28] Several studies highlight the efficacy of treating depression with exercise, with findings that it can be just as, if not even more, effective as psychotropic medication in treating moderate levels of depression.[29] Having a student participate in just 15 minutes of fun, cardio-based activity not only pays dividends physically but also promotes optimism following the release of the transmitter dopamine. Further, physical activity in school-age children is associated with improved self-regulation skills.[30]

The bottom line is that exercise is a valuable tool in the educators' arsenal to improve a student's emotional and academic functioning. Even better – it does not cost a penny! Please try to find a few minutes each day to incorporate physical activity, movement, or exercise into your classroom routine, particularly before exams or beginning a unit involving more complex concepts. This will go a long way to strengthening the student-teacher connection, as well as the substantive material covered in class.

Embrace Nature

Despite his life's work immersed in fact and science, theoretical physicist Albert Einstein, one of the greatest minds of all time, appreciated what nature provided to man's grasp of his world.

> Look deep into nature, and then you will understand everything better.[31]
>
> Albert Einstein, Theoretical physicist

Finding ways to help students connect with teachers and classmates consistently can be challenging. Many teachers have told me they feel like entertainers at times, between holding their students' attention and keeping them on task. An innovative way to help students develop their ability to pay attention is to take the act on the road – if possible, consider teaching lessons outside. Research shows that outdoor lessons can help students be more attentive and focused not only while outside, which may seem counterintuitive, but when they subsequently return to the indoor classroom. Teachers rate students as more engaged following an outdoor lesson[32,33] and noted that the number of times they needed to redirect students after an outdoor lesson was significantly less than those who had their previous lesson indoors.[34] In all instances, it should be understood that teachers must obtain prior permission from administrators and parents to hold outdoor lessons and provide adequate supervision at all times. Enlist the help of another teacher, an aide, a member of the administrative staff, or a parent, and remember that student safety remains the responsibility of the school – and the teacher.

Enhancing the applicability of this concept was that the students were not wandering around while outside. Instead, they were sitting still. As long as the students were in an area with some greenery, these effects were noted while they were outside during the lesson and continued after they returned to the classroom.[35]

Spending time in nature reduces stress, increases attention, and improves children's immune system functioning; in studies, students also reported feeling less stressed than their peers who did not go outside for lessons.[36] It is no surprise that calm children learn more effectively than stressed or agitated students. Outdoor classes improve students' intrinsic motivation to learn and develop a more positive attitude toward school. As today's increased academic demands are presented to children, especially as they go into higher grades, more rather than less outdoor time is needed. In one situation, a teacher set up an outdoor classroom during COVID restrictions and noticed a positive impact on his students. Not only did classroom participation increase markedly, but the students also reported positive feelings when class was held outside.[37]

Research shows that watching nature videos that focus on scenery rather than animals can also increase happiness and curiosity in students while decreasing anger and fatigue. Showing these videos indoors during class is a helpful alternative if it is not possible to go outside due to weather conditions, lack of access to a suitable or safe area, lack of additional supervision, or because the school administration has not pre-approved outdoor classes.[38] Additionally, these videos can be played during review and test-taking.

Researchers also found that children who felt connected to nature were more likely to engage in altruistic behavior, be more attuned to caring for the environment, and be happier.[39] Take your class outside to enjoy nature and allow them a few minutes to soak up the atmosphere. In addition, they can be encouraged to collect items such as twigs, grass, or stones to create a diorama or do an alphabet scavenger hunt in which each child looks for nature items that begin with a particular letter. Designating one minute of time outside to be one of silence in which your students pay attention to all the sounds they hear is also an excellent way to practice mindfulness.

Display Your Passion

Television personality from the popular show Shark Tank, Barbara Coran, said it best,

You can't fake passion.[40]

Perhaps one of the most powerful things you can do for your students is to get in touch with your passion for being a teacher and allow it to be on full display, observed, and shared by your students. Nothing piques someone's interest more than experiencing another's dedication and excitement for their craft. It is contagious and can inspire a desire to do more in our own life. Children are surprisingly capable of picking up on the emotional cues of others. Students who experience your love for what you do, whether directly in your relationship with them or through how you teach, will be positively impacted. Letting students see firsthand how deep your commitment to them is will promote greater classroom engagement overall. When students experience this, they will feel your excitement about teaching, energizing them further.

A recent study by the Gallup organization in which over 600,000 students were questioned about their school experiences had a remarkable finding.[41] Students who felt strongly that they had at least one teacher who made them "feel excited about the future" and that their school was "committed to building the strengths of each student" were over 30 times more likely to experience significantly greater engagement in the classroom than those students who disagreed with those statements. This greater degree of student engagement with their teachers was also associated with increased reading and math achievement levels.

One way to motivate your students is to have inspirational quotes displayed in the classroom. These can be in any manner you prefer – post quotes around the room, present students with new quotes each week, or write them on the board at the beginning of each class as the students come in when their attention is focused on what you are doing – and discuss them with your students. It does not matter if these quotes are from people who have achieved success, if the names are well known to the students, or if they are obscure. Ideas that convey determination, grit, and perseverance can be powerful messages and can influence students to consider different ways to pursue their goals. Locating such quotes should not be difficult, as a quick Google search will unearth thousands.

Quotes often open the eyes and the mind to truths and help us acknowledge and understand things we otherwise would have missed. They let us see life from another, broader perspective, and in this sense they expand the mind and awareness. Reading quotes can improve how you feel and change your mood. Exposing students to intriguing ideas in a quote can resonate with them for longer than it took to read the quote itself.

Providing students context about the quote, such as the source and background, can also be helpful to further fuel the student's motivation. For instance, you can briefly discuss the person whose quote you highlighted that day. If you are quoting Einstein, Lincoln, or Churchill, you can note that Albert Einstein was unable to figure out how to pay for things when his mother sent him to the store – today, he might be considered to have learning challenges. Abraham Lincoln was poverty-stricken early, went barefoot, and walked miles to borrow and return books from neighbors because his family only owned two books. Students will find it interesting (and some will find it reassuring and encouraging) that Winston Churchill, despite coming from the opposite type of childhood home as Lincoln, was a terrible student. In fact, he did not distinguish himself as a politician until he became the Prime Minister of Great Britain late in life when he was already a grandfather! Seeing how such figures overcame obstacles in their lives may make it easier for students to relate to them and be receptive to their message.

Promoting Self-Compassion in Students

Jack Kornfeld studied in Thailand after serving there in the Peace Corp and became a Buddhist Monk and expresses the value of self-compassion in this quote.

> If your compassion does not include yourself, it is incomplete.[42]

We have talked about how important it is for teachers to allow students to take risks and, if need be, fail. This allows them to learn from their experiences. Inherent in this notion is that students develop the capacity for self-compassion. Self-compassion is made up of three components: 1) Self-kindness – the ability to treat ourselves with caring, kindness, and compassion; 2) the feeling of being connected with others, rather than feeling alone; and 3) being able to accept and be aware of what we are experiencing without pushing it away. Students who lack this ability put themselves at risk for emotional and physical distress. Those who demonstrate this ability can have a healthier diet, better manage chronic pain, and be less likely to abuse drugs. Psychologically, self-compassionate students are less likely to experience depression and more likely to have stronger relationships while experiencing more significant levels of success at school.[43]

This can be especially important for your students to help them recover after any setbacks they may experience in class, whether a lower grade than they expected on a test, assignment, project, final grade received at the end of a semester, or a social faux pas. Teaching them or modeling self-compassion puts you in a position to help them recover from a difficult or challenging moment. Just as children are taught to accept the apology of others after someone else commits a transgression, this needs to also hold true for themselves. Parents spend a great deal of time teaching their children to be nice to others. How much time is spent communicating to children that it is equally important to do the same for themselves? Without this input, it can become difficult for a child to give themself a break when needed instead of becoming hypercritical and perfectionistic, which will impact a student's performance in the classroom and throughout life. Emphasizing achievement without self-kindness puts students at risk for burnout.

To introduce this concept to children, ask if they can come up with an example of a time they tried to help a friend who was upset or worried feel better after a setback. Perhaps it was in the classroom, on the athletic field, or following a disagreement with a friend or parent. Ask your students what they said to their friend to make them feel better, then suggest that they might use the exact words or phrases to make themselves feel better after they fail at something or suffer a disappointment.

Discuss how they handle making mistakes or witness how their peers deal with making errors. Ask them to share what they hear others say in such instances, citing examples of negative quotes to introduce the idea that using such words can make everyone feel unhappy, even making them want to give up. Then engage your class in brainstorming alternative, positive words they can use for themselves or a friend to help them feel better when they make a mistake. You can provide students with examples of self-compassion phrases they can use, such as "I am learning," "Everyone makes mistakes," and "I tried my best." You may also have them share situations in which they became angry with themselves for making mistakes and suggest how using phrases such as those above could have helped at that moment.

Once the class understands the concept, you can invite them to write a self-compassion letter.[44] This involves five short steps and can take around 15 minutes.

Because it is easier to offer kindness to others or think about others' kindness than to offer that compassion to ourselves, have the students think about someone in their life who is kind to them before writing the letter. Have the students write down a shortcoming or flaw that bothers them about themself. Next, have them write the name of a person in their life who shows them compassion and kindness. Then have the student list words this person has used in the past to show they understand and care about them. Ask the student to imagine the words that person might say to them to make them feel better about something. The student can then write a letter that explores their emotional reactions to this situation. Do not have students concern themselves with grammar or spelling; this exercise is designed to help them begin to learn the importance of engaging in self-compassionate behavior.

If this assignment is too challenging for students based on their age or skill level, suggest writing a love letter to themselves. They can highlight their strengths as well as things they can do better. Teachers can model this for their students.

Helping students become more understanding and kinder to themselves will help them display such behavior toward others and navigate challenging situations without getting down on themselves. Self-compassion is a way to foster well-being and an effective antidote to self-criticism.

Accentuate the Positive

Legendary musician and songwriter Willie Nelson took some time finding his niche in the music world. Despite setbacks he persevered. His philosophy may explain why he eventually found success.

Once you replace negative thoughts with positive ones, you'll start having positive results.[45]

Our words carry a great deal of weight and can impact others in a significant way. This was illustrated in a study performed by two psychologists, Barbara Frederickson and Marcial Losada, to determine how communication can create productive, efficient teams in the business world. These researchers came up with a positivity ratio, which compares positive to negative comments.[46] For Frederickson and Losada, the optimal ratio was three positive comments for every negative comment from a supervisor. This ratio distinguished high-performing business teams from lower-performing ones.

Due to methodological difficulties, the authors later recanted some of their findings.[47] Other investigators, however, pursued studying the thesis[48] and found that one of the main differences between high-performing and low-performing business teams was a positivity ratio of 5:1. Medium-performing teams had a ratio of just under 2:1, and low-performing teams had a ratio of less than 1:1.

The inclusion of some negative feedback, however, is critical. For one thing, it certainly gets the attention of the person it is directed toward. Second, negative feedback prevents complacency. It can force people to rethink their ideas, leading to improvement or a new perspective. By presenting negative feedback alongside positive feedback in the ratio of 5:1, performance can markedly improve.

When I first came across the concept of a positivity ratio, it was applied strictly to corporate teams. However, I immediately wondered if these findings could be generalized to other relationships, such as teacher-student and parent-child. I suggested that the parents and teachers I worked with use the ratio as a rule of thumb in their interactions with children. With some instruction on how to provide appropriate and respectful feedback, parents embraced this strategy. They reported a significant improvement in their child's behavior and relationship with each other.

In applying this concept in schools, positive feedback must be realistic to the task at hand. Providing vague, overly inflated feedback ("you are the greatest") not tied to a specific outcome lacks impact. It likely will not lead to behavioral changes – students will know when a teacher is exaggerating, which will detract from any positive effect the praise might have. Keep the positive feedback tied to what was accomplished, making it behavioral-based. To increase the power of the feedback, try to deliver it as close in time as possible to when the event happened. While negative feedback should always be delivered privately, positive feedback can be delivered in front of a group if you feel that other students can also benefit.

The positivity ratio need not be limited to providing feedback. The comments can include such feedback as "you worked so hard on that," "thanks for getting that homework done in time," or "it took a lot of courage to answer that tough question." In other situations, you can use cheerful greetings at the start of the school day or after breaks, such as "I am so happy to see everyone," and "Welcome back," or check in with students with benign questions like "Did you walk to school today? It was really cold!" or "How was your vacation?" You can follow up on a student's hobbies or interests by asking, "How did the band concert go last night?" or "I know you are such a huge baseball fan. Did you see the game yesterday?" In addition, you can have positive nonverbal interactions with students, such as when you smile at them, give a thumbs up, or nod, indicating reasonable effort.

Try to find something positive and reflect it to the student. If it is genuinely challenging to find enough examples of positive behavior, start small and gradually build up. You can say that you are happy to see them when they arrive at school and reinforce even the slightest effort they make. You can even thank them for paying attention.

If students feel embarrassed or uncomfortable receiving praise, try to follow the 5:1 ratio with other students. Students will experience this as part of the class norm. If they are still very uncomfortable receiving verbal praise, jot down a brief note to give to them or include particular praise on a paper or test. Even body language, such as a smile, can go a long way.

Research shows that the use of the 5:1 ratio in the classroom can enhance students' academic engagement. Better-behaved students will feel appreciated and have an improved classroom environment.[49,50]

Like many strategies rooted in a strength-based framework, this free, easy-to-use method can provide a considerable upside for students and teachers. Interestingly, in a study in which teachers received the positivity ratio from administrators, the teachers reported greater engagement in their job and a more significant amount of positive emotion.[51]

Share Your Growth

An anonymous but wise person stated,

> The courage it takes to share your story might be the very thing someone else needs to open their heart to hope.[52]

Having the opportunity to share everyday experiences with others pays dividends for everyone. Indeed, it can promote a sense of belonging. As teachers, we have a wealth of experiences past and present that our students could relate to and, more importantly, learn from. Sharing with your students the various twists and turns your life has taken can inspire them. I am not suggesting that very personal experiences be shared; personal boundaries must be adhered to in all cases. However, if a student knows their teacher went through circumstances similar to those they are going through and found a way to cope, it provides hope.

Life can be described as many things: a journey, a story, an adventure, or an ongoing series of experiences. However you describe it, life is full of moments that turn into memories. Some of the memories are great, and others are not-so-great. Either way, these moments helped us become who we are today. One significant thing about memories is that they can be shared.

Students who experience you as enhancing their level of engagement and as someone who has something more to offer than solely dispensing knowledge will deepen their relationship with you. Pupils may be more likely to seek you out when they are going through challenges, which could impact their classroom performance, making them more receptive to your ideas and suggestions.

Sharing personal stories about our past and present can be done informally. They can be sprinkled into lessons. Do not be afraid, within reason, to share areas where you have felt vulnerable. This can be from an academic or social perspective. Students will get to know you as not a "know-it-all" but rather as a fellow human being who does not have all the answers. I have, for example, shared my struggles with tenth-grade math – that I failed it twice before ultimately succeeding. In that instance, it improved the rapport the student and I had, while communicating that failure could be OK. It also encouraged them to share their feelings about their own experiences.

Research shows that learners who feel connected to their teachers and classmates have higher levels of achievement than their less-connected peers.[53] Allowing ourselves to reveal our shortcomings and imperfections by telling our own stories communicates to students that we are, in fact, more like them than they may imagine and make us less intimidating to them. This builds trust, which is crucial, especially when you have difficult conversations with your students. As you listen to your students, they will listen in return. Allow them to get to know you as a person, not just their teacher.

In deciding to share personal stories with students, keep the following points in mind: Share only appropriate stories that have a connection to the classroom; tell stories that create common ground with your students; share stories that help students understand that worry is universal. Be sure to include stories about how you solved a problem that students might face so you can help them move forward to find solutions of their own. Tell stories that illustrate resilience and courage. You are a role model for your students, and seeing your strength will inspire them to persevere and stand up for what they believe in. Remember not to share current problems so as not to worry them or make them feel like they are somehow responsible for fixing them.

Classroom Exercises to Help Your Students Discover Their Strengths

Revered French novelist, Marcel Proust, encouraged the reader to see the present with a different perspective.

> The only real voyage of discovery exists, not in seeing new landscapes, but in having new eyes.[54]
>
> Marcel Proust, Author

In a strength-based model, we look for a student to thrive, not merely survive. Becoming aware of their competencies, especially after believing they did not have any, can be an incredibly liberating and empowering experience for students. It gives them the confidence to spread their wings, try new things, and even risk making mistakes. Most importantly, having your students connect to their strengths can instill hope. As President Theodore Roosevelt said, "Do what you can, with what you have, where you are."[55]

When I meet a child for the first time, I try to engage the child in discussing what they feel is their strength. This helps build an alliance with children. Even if a child tells me they cannot think of anything they do well, I respond, "It's OK if you can't think of anything, everyone has something they are good at, and one of our goals is to figure out what that is."

Unsurprisingly, students who are aware of their strengths and tap into them have been shown to experience higher happiness levels and feel less depressed and anxious than their peers who do not believe they have strengths. Helping students discover their capabilities in a fun way will enhance their relationship with you and boost their motivation to do well in school.

Classroom teachers can help their students discover their hidden assets by pointing out what they do well and emphasizing their successes. This helps children begin to appreciate themselves. However, helping kids identify strengths does not have to rest solely on the feedback they receive from you. You can introduce fun exercises to your class to help them begin to discover for themselves what buried (and maybe some not-so-buried) treasures they possess. Below are some of the best strength-based exercises I have used.

A relatively easy activity is to have an accomplishment box for each student in the classroom.[56] The purpose of the box is to allow children to look back over the things they have accomplished. All you need is an empty tissue box covered with colored paper and other decorations. Students can be given a supply of index cards or, if you like, make an accomplishment sheet divided into several columns. You will need at least two sheets of paper with columns labeled with different categories such as school, activities, social skills, and home. Ask students leading questions to get them to brainstorm, such as: "What are you proud of?" "What have you improved the most at?" and "What shows how hard you have worked?" The student can fill in some answers in each column, cut them out, and put them in their accomplishment box. This is a practical, concrete way for children to see their accomplishments increase and take a trip down memory lane to reinforce their successes, especially if they come up against a frustrating situation.

Another exercise that is beneficial in helping students identify their assets is the strength chain. The instructions and template can be downloaded with the link noted in the references.[57] The child is presented with a list of strengths in seven different areas: character, social, language, reading, math, logic, and study skills, as well as lists of other strengths and talents. The students go through the rather exhaustive list and cut out the sentences on the sheets that apply to them or create their own and then color them in and make a chain. The student's chains can be hung from the wall or strung together and talked about in class. The point is that everyone has individual strengths, and when they are pooled, the group is stronger.

A fun way to help children think about their strengths is a sentence completion exercise filled out by the teacher. This strategy forces teachers to consider the assets of their students from a variety of angles. Some sample sentences are as follows as seen in template developed by www.yourtherapysource. com.[58]

1. This student is best at _____
2. This student has a fantastic ability to _____
3. This student is frequently recognized for _____
4. This student smiles when _____
5. This student is happiest when _____
6. This student participates the most when_____
7. This student does _____ better than any other student in class.
8. This student is highly interested in _____
9. This student is highly motivated by _____
10. This student always takes pride in his/her work when _____

(www.yourtherapysource.com/blog1/2019/08/26/student-strengths-in-the-classroom-2/.)

The information gathered from this exercise can be used in your student assessment and shared with parents either in a note sent home or during parent-teacher conferences.

The "Who Am I?" Flowchart,[59] developed by educators Leyton Schnellert and Pat Miranda (Figure 5.1), can be an easy way for students to identify their assets and share them with the class. Getting your student's perspective on what they do well can give you a tremendous head start in formulating strategies that can impact your students in a more personally relevant manner.

Another intriguing tool to help students tune into their strengths is the Identity Tree designed by Wejr and Copeland[60] (Figure 5.2). The template is reproduced below. An additional wrinkle in this exercise is that it helps students not only zero-in on their assets but also think about their impact on others.

Who am I? Profile

Some words that describe me are....		
My favourite books/stories are...	Some things I like to do with my friend are...	My favourite activities that I do on my own are...
My favourite activities I do with my family are...	I am very good at/ or interested in...	Some hopes and dreams that I have for myself are...
Some important things that you should/ or need to know about me are...	The easiest way for me to show what I know is...	Something I would like to get better at this year is...
Some of my greatest fears are...		

FIGURE 5.1 Who Are the Students? (Leyton Schnellert)
A Flow Chart to Identify Student Strengths

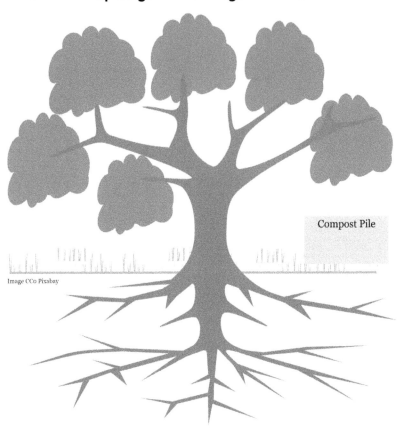

#StartwithStrengths
January 25, 2017
Chris Wejr
Karen Copeland

Exploring Our Own Strengths and Talents

Compost Pile

Image CC0 Pixabay

Completing Your Tree

Roots: Where you come from - Location, Culture, Heritage

Trunk: Tall, Flexible and Strong - Your Strengths and Talents

Branches: Reaching Out - Goals, Hopes and Dreams

Leaves: Those around you who are significant to you and affected by your strengths and talents

Compost Pile (*Optional): Those areas that we were once defined by that we refuse to be defined by now

Soil: Actions to put your strengths to use

Identity Tree Activity via https://app.classkick.com/#/assignments/AVj5qsbLSC26gZ8_uvUqPA

FIGURE 5.2 Exploring Our Own Strengths and Talents
Tree Diagram Highlighting Student Strengths

Mountain of Strengths is a technique developed by Dr. David Crenshaw,[61] a noted psychologist and play therapist. This technique can be used individually or in a group setting. Using an 8.5 x 11 (inches) piece of paper, you or your student can outline a mountain leaving the interior blank. During the week, each student adds one talent or strength starting at the bottom of the mountain, eventually filling it up to the top. The student can be called upon to talk about the strength they chose. When they get to the top, the mountain will have been filled with their list of strengths and talents, and you and your student can take turns summarizing them. If your student is stuck and cannot come up with anything, you can suggest possible talents for them to think about. Hold a classroom party when the class fills up each mountain to celebrate their capabilities.

A counseling activity that can be used in the classroom is to ask the student to draw an award for him or herself. It can be filled in any way they want. Following this, you can ask the child why they deserve the award. What will they do with it? Have they won any other awards, and if so, for what? Ask any further questions you devise to further the discussion. If students have difficulty doing this, you can pair them up or place them in a small group to create awards for each other.

One strategy that can be used is to ask students to do a drawing or collage, highlighting attributes about themselves that they admire and offer the students examples of possible traits they can use. The drawings can be used as a springboard for discussion. Students can describe their strengths and give examples when they have utilized them. If it is easier, they can use pictures from magazines or printed from the web.

Another exercise is to have students draw strengths growing from the ground in the form of flowers or plants and label them. Discuss what strengths they picked, their favorites, and how to help the flowers (strengths) grow, as was illustrated in using the tree as previously noted. If several students do this, all the drawings can be hung on the wall to have a whole garden of strengths.

A popular strategy I use with children in therapy sessions is a Thumball®.[62] These are vinyl balls that come in different sizes and themes. The balls are divided into sections with words or graphics related to a specific topic. The ball is thrown back and forth between two or more students. After catching the ball, the student looks under their thumb to see what it says and begins to talk about it. If the student needs help, the teacher may read it to them. The ball is handy in facilitating a therapeutic conversation on various topics such as emotions, likes and dislikes, values, or general icebreakers. In this context, it can promote discussion about student strengths.

While a Thumball® is commercially available, if you prefer, you can make a custom ball by using a sponge or vinyl ball and dividing it into different sections. Write a quality, talent, or trait in each section, such as planning, reading, setting goals, listening, and self-control. When someone catches it, they give an example of when they used that asset. If they cannot respond, another participant can say when they saw the student use that particular talent.

A group exercise that lends itself nicely to working with students in a strength-based way is to give each student an index card with their name on one side. The cards are then passed around the group. On the reverse side of the card, each student writes as many positive things they can think about the person named on the front of the card; after one minute, the card is given to the person next to them. After the cards make their way around the entire group, collect them and hand out a card to each student, ensuring no one gets their own card. Have each student look at each card, create an award for the person listed on the card, and present the award they create for that student by giving a short speech about their peer's assets.

This selection of activities can be instrumental in helping students not only identify their hidden assets but can also enhance their self-esteem. Having their strengths validated can go a long way to improving motivation and engagement. The point is to provide students with the structure to raise awareness of their strengths and find ways to put these strengths to use. The ideas presented are relatively inexpensive or free, easy to implement, fun, and engaging for you and your students.

This chapter illustrates how a student's strengths can be identified and accessed in a wide variety of ways. Teachers are only limited by their imagination!

References

1. Hallowell, N. (2001). *Connect: 12 Vital Ties That Open Your Heart, Lengthen Your Life and Deepen Your Soul*. Gallery Books.
2. Selva, J. (2021, March 21). "76 most powerful mindfulness quotes: Your daily dose of inspiration." *Positive Psychology.com* https://positivepsychology.com/mindfulness-quotes/
3. David Lynch Foundation for Consciousness-Based Education and World Peace. www.davidlynchfoundation.org/message.html
4. David Lynch Foundation. (2013) *Health and Quality of Life Outcomes*. (2003). 1:10.
5. David Lynch Foundation. (2011) *Education*, 131, 556–565.
6. David Lynch Foundation. (2013) *Education*, 133(4), 495–500.
7. Modesto-Lowe, V. Farahmand, P. Chaplin, M., & Sarro, L. (2015, December, 22). "Does mindfulness meditation improve attention in attention deficit hyperactivity disorder?" *World Journal of Psychiatry*, 397–403.
8. David Lynch Foundation. (2001) *Intelligence*, 29, 419–440.
9. Nidich, S.I., Rainforth, M., Haaga, D., Hagelin, J., &Salerno, J. (2009, December). "A randomized controlled trial on effects of the transcendental meditation program on blood pressure, psychological distress, and coping in young adults." *American Journal of Hypertension* 22(12), 1326–1331.
10. Elder, C., Nidich, S., Moriarty, F., & Nidich, R. (2014, March 1). "Effect of transcendental meditation on employee stress, depression and burnout: A randomized controlled study." *Permanente Journal*, 18(1), 19–23.
11. Beach, S. (2014. July 23; 2017, December 6). "8 ways to teach mindfulness to kids." *Huffpost*. bit.ly/3JbuT1U
12. Khoury, E. (2019, August 5). "Mindfulness: An approach to better self-esteem and mental health for children and teenagers." *Curious*

Neuron. www.curiousneuron.com/learningarticles/2019/7/22/mindfulness-an-approach-to-better-self-esteem-and-mental-health-for-children-and-teenagers

13. Weare, K. (2012, April). "Evidence for the impact of mindfulness on children and young people. the mindfulness in schools project, in association with the University Of Exeter." https://mindfulnessinschools.org/wp-content/uploads/2013/02/MiSP-Research-Summary-2012.pdf
14. Goleman, D. (2013) "Breathing buddies video on YouTube." https://youtu.be/scqFHGI_nZE
15. Kumar, K. (2021, November 18). "Why do U.S. Navy SEALS use box breathing?" *MedicineNet*. www.medicinenet.com/why_do_navy_seals_use_box_breathing/article.htm
16. Paquette, J. (2018). *The Happiness Toolbox*. Pesi.
17. The Education Magazine. (2022) "10 quotes of physical education to harness a happy future." www.theeducationmagazine.com/word-art/10-quotes-physical-education/
18. Kipner, S. & Shaddick, T. (1981). Physical. (Song). Olivia Newton-John. MCA Records.
19. www.cdc.gov/physicalactivity/basics/pa-health/index.htm
20. http://pediatrictherapies.com/exercise-brain-exercise-can-improve-academic-performance-child/
21. U.S. Department of Health and Human Services, Centers for Disease Control and Prevention, National Center for Chronic Disease Prevention and Health Promotion, & Division of Adolescent and School Health. (rev. July, 2010). The Association Between School-Based Physical Activity, Including Physical Education and Academic Performance www.cdc.gov/healthyyouth/health_and_academics/pdf/pape_executive_summary.pdf. June 2010
22. Ibid.
23. Mitchell, M. (2004). "Physically fit children appear to do better in the classroom, researchers say." University of Illinois. https://news.illinois.edu/view/6367/207471
24. Mountain Heights Academy. (2020). "Exercising to improve your grades." https://mountainheightsacademy.org/exercising-to-improve-your-grades
25. "Physical Activity Enables Higher Grades." (2021, September). *Monitor On Psychology*, 52(6), 17.

26. Viadero, D. (2008, February 13). "Exercise seen as priming pump for students' academic strides." *Education Week*. www.healthaffairs. org/do/10.1377/hblog20140207.037053/full/

27. Ratey, J. & Hagerman, E. (2008). *Spark: The Revolutionary New Science of Exercise and The Brain*. Little, Brown & Company.

28. Mozes, A. (2021, September 13). "Anxious? Maybe you can exercise it away." *HealthDay*. Tweet by American Psychological Association. https://consumer.healthday.com/9-13-anxious-maybe-you-can-exercise-it-away-2654939173.html

29. Bergland, C. (2013, October, 29). "25 studies confirm: Exercise prevents depression." *Psychology Today*. www.psychologytoday. com/us/blog/the-athletes-way/201310/25-studies-confirm-exercise-prevents-depression

30. Physical Activity Enables Higher Grades. (2021, September). *Monitor On Psychology*. 52(6), 17.

31. Albert Einstein Quotes. (2022). *BrainQuote*. www.brainyquote.com/quotes/albert_einstein_106912

32. Briggs, S. (2018, February 12). "Outdoor learning boosts student engagement." *Informed*. www.opencolleges.edu.au/informed/features/outdoor-learning-boosts-student-engagement/

33. Suttie, J. (2018, May 14). "The surprising benefits of teaching a class outside." *Greater Good Magazine*. https://greatergood.berkeley.edu/article/item/the_surprising_benefits_of_teaching_a_class_outside

34. Reuters. (2021, April 12). "Children swap classrooms for beach lessons in Spain." *New York Post*.

35. Suttie, J. (2018, May 14). "The surprising benefits of teaching a class outside." *Greater Good Magazine*. https://greatergood.berkeley.edu/article/item/the_surprising_benefits_of_teaching_a_class_outside

36. Dewar, G. (2018). "Outdoor learning and green time: How kids benefit from learning and playing in nature." *Parenting Science*. https://parentingscience.com/outdoor-learning/

37. Young, S. (2021, August 16). "This teacher's outdoor classroom during covid inspired a wave of others: 'We saw a change in students.'" https://people.com/human-interest/nicholas-dixon-outdoor-classroom-hero-teache/

38. Tanvi, J. (2021, May 22). "Watching nature on TV & VR boosts your wellbeing, according to new study." *Green Queen*. www.greenqueen.com.hk/watching-nature-on-tv-vr-boosts-your-wellbeing-according-to-new-study/

39. Gander, K. (2020, February 26). "Children who feel connected to nature likely to be happier, study suggests." *Newsweek*. www.newsweek.com/children-who-feel-connected-nature-likely-happier-study-suggests-1488738

40. Kerpen, D. (2014, March 27) "Inspiring quotes on passion get back to what you love." *Inc.* www.inc.com/dave-kerpen/15-quotes-on-passion-to-inspire-a-better-life.html

41. Blad, E. (2014) "More than half of students engaged in school, says poll." *Education Week*. www.edweek.org/leadership/more-than-half-of-students-engaged-in-school-says-poll/2014/04#:~:text=Students%20who%20strongly%20agree%20that,signs%20of%20engagement%20in%20the

42. "15 Quotes … About Quotes!" (2016, June, 8*). Storyzy* https://medium.com/@storyzy/15-quotes-about-quotes-36897f50377d

43. Guerra, J. (2018, November 17). "Empower your students with self-compassion." *Mindful Schools*. www.mindfulschools.org/inspiration/empower-students-with-self-compassion/

44. Paquette, J. (2018). *The Happiness Toolbox*. Pesi Publishing.

45. Arlen, Harold and Mercer, Johnny. (1944). Ac-Cent-Tchu-Ate-The Positive. (Song). Capital Records. Performed by Bing Crosby & The Andrew Sisters.

46. Fredrickson, B. & Losada, M. (2005). "Positive affect and the complex dynamics of human flourishing." *American Psychologist*, 60(7), 678–686. https://doi.org/10.1037/0003-066X.60.7.678

47. Brown, N., Sokal, A., & Friedman, H. (2014). "Positive psychology and romantic scientism." *American Psychologist*, 69(6), 636–637. https://doi.org/10.1037/a0037390

48. Ryerse, M. (2017, February 6). "School culture and relationships thrive with A 5:1 positivity ratio." www.gettingsmart.com/2017/02/culture-relationships-positivity-ratio/

49. Ibid.

50. Sparks, S. (2019, March 12). "Why teacher-student relationships matter." *Education Week*. www.edweek.org/teaching-learning/why-teacher-student-relationships-matter/2019/03

51. Rusu, P. & Colomeischi, A. (2020, July). "Positivity ratio and well-being among teachers: The mediating role of work engagement." *Frontiers in Psychology*, 11, www.frontiersin.org/article/10.3389/fpsyg.2020.01608

52. Healey, J. (2018, November, 23). "20 quotes about sharing your story: Baring your heart & healing hurts." *Healing Brave* https://healingbrave.com/blogs/all/quotes-about-sharing-your-story

53. Blair, L. (2018, May 17). "The psychological benefits of shared experiences." *The Telegraph*. www.telegraph.co.uk/health-fitness/mind/psychological-benefits-shared-experiences/

54. "Marcel Proust Quotes" (2022). *BrainyQuote*. bit.ly/3Hp7Eju

55. "Theodore Roosevelt Quotes" (2022). BrainyQuote. www.brainyquote.com/quotes/theodore_roosevelt_100965

56. The Understood Team. Your Child's Accomplishment Box Starter Kit. https://assets.ctfassets.net/p0qf7j048i0q/36R8Wpo0WlzUlwDsxLALvV/574b7ea0302403c3b7f990b14942e3fb/Your_Child___s_Accomplishment_Box_Starter_Kit_Understood.pdf

57. Morin, A. (2022). "Strengths chain: Hands-on activity to help kids identify their strengths." *Understood*. www.understood.org/en/friends-feelings/empowering-your-child/building-on-strengths/strengths-chain-for-kids

58. "Finding Student's Strengths In The Classroom." (2019)/ *Your Therapy Source*. www.yourtherapysource.com/blog1/2019/08/26/student-strengths-in-the-classroom-2/

59. (Reproduced with permission.) Schnellert, L., Watson, L., & Widdess, N. (2015). *It's All About Thinking: Creating Pathways for All Learners in the Middle Years*. Portage & Main Press.

60. http://chriswejr.com/2015/04/19/10-ways-to-determine-the-strengths-of-our-students/

61. Crenshaw, D. (2006). *Evocative Strategies in Child And Adolescent Psychotherapy*. Jason Aronson Publisher.

62. www.thumball.com/

6

How To Become a
Strength-Based Teacher

Children are remarkably perceptive about how their teachers perceive them as proven by this student.

> My teacher thought I was smarter than I was. So I was.[1]
>
> A six-year-old student

What inspired you to become a teacher? Was it a calling? An opportunity to fulfill a long-held desire to work with children? Was it based on practical considerations such as the length of the academic calendar and school day? Whatever your primary motivation, you are now part of what has been called a "noble profession."[2] You have the opportunity to impact the heart, soul, and mind of a child. A rather heady responsibility indeed! However, the initial excitement of your career choice may have lost some of its luster. This could be due to a variety of circumstances beyond your control. These can include:

- ♦ changes in your job duties and role since you entered the field;
- ♦ having to contend with increasingly larger classes than you anticipated;

DOI: 10.4324/9781003368014-7

- ◆ changes in the curriculum you may not be happy about;
- ◆ the increased importance of assessments;
- ◆ feeling unappreciated;
- ◆ feeling disrespected;
- ◆ not making as much money as you would like; and
- ◆ experiencing too much stress or fatigue from dealing with workplace politics.

A survey of 166 teachers in Australia between the ages of 22–65 conducted before the COVID pandemic in 2020 revealed that approximately half the teachers in the sample reported feeling significantly depressed and anxious.[3] Nearly 18 percent of the respondents had symptoms that met moderate to severe depression criteria, while 62 percent met moderate to severe anxiety criteria. Fifty-six percent met the diagnostic criteria of medium to high severity of having physical symptoms such as chest pains and panic attacks. In addition, 17 percent were at risk for probable alcohol or drug abuse. These rates were all significantly higher than the national average. Data suggests this trend may not be limited to Australia, as other countries report up to three times higher rates of alcohol abuse for teachers than the general population. In a survey of American schoolteachers, 45 percent agreed with the statement: "I do not seem to have as much enthusiasm now as I did when I began teaching."[4]

Embracing a strength-based philosophy can mitigate these outcomes. Helping children discover their strengths does not just provide benefits for students – it is a process that allows teachers to grow while renewing their commitment to the profession. Choosing not to focus primarily on what is wrong with a child lessens hopelessness for everyone in the classroom, including the teacher. The strengths-based teacher does not ignore challenges but instead looks for ways to attack them using the strengths of the individual student.

Becoming a strength-based teacher can inspire your students while also reigniting the spark that initially led to you becoming a teacher. Planting the seeds of success for students will provide you with enhanced job satisfaction and perhaps greater love for what you do. It will be constructive to consider the following points to boost or recapture your enthusiasm to teach.

Connect With Your Story of Origin

Danish existential philosopher Soren Kierkegaard noted

> You live life looking forward. You understand life looking backward.[5]

Sometimes it is helpful to take a step back and retrace how you arrived at your present destination. Embracing your story of origin can help accomplish this. Origin is defined as something that "applies to the things or persons from which something is ultimately derived and often to the causes operating before the thing itself comes into being."[6] Taking a trip back in time can be helpful in understanding and coping with present-day challenges.

This is not just retracing the concrete steps that led to your present position, such as what education classes you took in college or what you liked or disliked about your mentors in graduate school. Instead, it is looking back on what inspired you to go into teaching. What thoughts, ideas, and feelings fueled your desire to teach? It is easy to get so caught up in the day-to-day routine of what we do that we forget to get off the merry-go-round and reflect.

Often what we imagined at the start of our professional journey changes due to many twists and turns along the way, some expected, some not. Sometimes it can help to write down notes about how this process unfolded. Be sure to include the conversations you had with others that led to your considering teaching and immerse yourself in the evolution of how this came to be. Examples of things to reflect on include: Was your mom or dad a teacher, and did you want to follow in their footsteps? Did you like to play school with your stuffed animals as captive students? Did you have a favorite TV show about teachers and school that made you think it would be an interesting, fun, or dramatic profession? Did you have a particularly inspiring teacher at a pivotal time in your life, or did you recognize how much more you would have enjoyed school if you'd had a teacher who inspired you? Did you base your decision along practical lines such as "there will always be a need for teachers, so I will always be able to find a job even in a different city"? Do you recall that "aha" moment when you knew this was what you wanted to do?

After some reflection, think about how your feelings may have changed. If so, when did those changes occur? What were the circumstances in your life when your feelings changed? For instance, did you have an unexpected change in grade assignment that turned out to be challenging? Were you assigned a class that was difficult to manage? Did you begin to feel pressure to teach to assessments, thus robbing you of creativity? Were such things beyond your control? In contrast, are there still aspects of your job that allow you to reconnect with your original hopes and expectations?

In attempting to reconnect with your origin story, do not be too quick to dismiss your state of mind or life circumstances when you initially decided to be a teacher. It seemed like a good idea at the time, and you did not doubt yourself. Your present-day circumstances do not invalidate your story of origin. Choosing to become a teacher came out of your hopes and dreams, experiences, struggles, and achievements. Reliving those feelings and experiences will help take you back to the teacher you wanted. Perhaps that will allow you to find ways to get back to being that person and that teacher.

Here are a few specific steps to create your story of origin.

♦ Ponder what in yourself, your family, or your background led you to consider becoming a teacher. Look back on your roots and try to tap into them.
♦ Consider your motivations for why you teach. Are these in line with what you initially thought about when you took the plunge into teaching?
♦ Decide if you are willing to continue fighting for what you want if you believe your situation may not be tenable. This may require you to dig deep and have an honest

conversation with yourself. Do not be afraid to have that conversation – it will be worth it!

◆ Determine if you feel confident that you can think about how you may need to find better or maybe just different ways to discover what you need from teaching.

The point is not to get caught up in the here and now, which will make you feel helpless, especially if any of your reasons for questioning your devotion to the field are due to circumstances beyond your control. Instead, look back at what was inside you that led you to become a teacher.

Interestingly, the term "Story of Origin" came into use when comic book publishers created backstories about how their superheroes attained their powers with additional details added to flesh out the story. Use the story of origin technique to help you connect to your superpowers and become the educator you set out to be and still want to be!

A slightly different way to compose your story can include the following steps.

◆ Think about your current situation and what your strengths and expertise are. It might help to jot these down and make a list.

◆ Go back in time to write about the episode in your life where your story begins. Think of three or four critical anecdotes in your life and write about how you navigated them from beginning to end.

◆ Reflect on the anecdotes you wrote about. Give some thought to how you feel and think now about what you felt and thought at that time.

◆ Move on to the next anecdote. Doing so will help you move forward and allow you to reconnect with your superpowers.

Getting in touch with your story of origin, of what inspired you to become a teacher, keeps you grounded to do your best to live up to your ideals. Once we become disillusioned with our ideals, we need to find a way to stay true to that part of ourselves that wants to teach and influence kids. We need to get back in touch with that part of ourselves we lost touch with or forgot about over the years.

Personal Control (Wriggle Room)

Roman Emperor and philosopher, Marcus Aurelius, knew a thing or two about power as evidenced in this quote.

> You have power over your mind – not outside events.
> Realize this, and you will find strength.[7]
>> Marcus Aurelius, Roman Emperor, philosopher

Larger class sizes, increased administrative responsibilities, and demanding parents are just a few examples of the variables you may have to contend with as a teacher in today's classroom. You probably will not have vast control over these things, adding to the challenge. Despite your feelings, these situations will still exist, so how do you cope with these challenges and prevent them from impacting your teaching ability?

In some instances, the unfortunate reality may be that you can do nothing to change these external challenges that can impact your classroom. While this may sound like you have to resign yourself to a situation and become resentful, Dr. Robert Brooks, a well-known psychologist who has studied resilience extensively, writes:

> One of the main characteristics of resilient people is that they focus on and act upon what they have control over, devoting little time or energy to factors that are beyond their sphere of influence. The courage to take responsibility and ownership for our actions requires that we recognize that we are the authors of our own lives. Resilient people do not pursue their happiness by asking or waiting for someone else to change first but rather consider, "What is it that I can do differently to change the situation?"[8]

There is a great deal of wisdom in these words. Holding onto negative feelings about things that upset us will not change the situation. It will only increase our stress levels and impact our mental and physical health. Sometimes we must acknowledge that certain realities will not change and must be accepted no matter how we feel.

Suppose something can be changed, then consider how that change can be made, even if only in a small way. This is much more helpful than ruminating over the problem. Evidence confirms that repeatedly going over something in our heads impacts our well-being. According to at least one study, the lack of control a person perceives they have over their job can be directly correlated to heart disease.[9]

In discussing this concept, Dr. Brooks reflected on a presentation he made to teachers when he asked what would help them be less stressed in their job. The teachers responded by citing a list of concerns, such as students coming from less dysfunctional families and coming to school more prepared to learn. While these may indeed be appropriate items for a wish list, they were things teachers could not control. Instead, Brooks suggests teachers consider how the school environment can help poorly prepared students be more motivated and cooperative – more ready to learn when they get to school. Looking at things from this perspective can reduce stress and help engender feelings of empowerment in the teacher as they seek new solutions.[10]

An exercise suggested by Dr. Brooks is to list three or four things you would like to see changed in your life. Then, review each item, asking yourself the following question: "For me to achieve this change, does someone else need to change first?" If the answer is yes, shift your time and energy to those items that do not require someone else to initiate (or participate in) the change. This can be the first step to taking responsibility for initiating change in your life.[11]

After gaining a sense of personal control, make sure the goals you are working toward are realistic. Are your ideals aligned with the reality you have to face? If not, it is time for self-evaluation to help reconsider what you are working toward. If I am blocked from getting to where I want to go, I need to think about another way to get there, to get around the thing blocking my progress in achieving my goal. Rethinking the destination is necessary if we are not making headway.

Having unrealistic goals can sabotage your attempts to succeed and lead to frustration. Instead, having goals that coincide with what you can realistically accomplish is essential for several additional reasons.

- ◆ Having goals provides focus and allows you to direct your efforts toward a specific end rather than disjointed and random attempts at an ill-defined outcome. As a result, your attention will be more closely aligned with your priorities.
- ◆ Setting a goal will help you assess your degree of progress. Without setting realistic goals, how do you know if what you are working toward is attainable and whether you are making progress? Setting goals should include creating benchmarks to evaluate progress along the way.
- ◆ Having goals will keep you motivated.
- ◆ Having goals will help reduce procrastination.
- ◆ Achieving a goal motivates you to achieve even more.

If you feel like you are spinning your wheels in your current role, give thought to the direction you are going.

Creativity

Sir Ken Robinson was a noted authority on education recognized by the Queen of England for his service, observed,

> Creativity now is as important in education as literacy, and we should treat it with the same status.[12]

One strategy to help add an element of personal control to your work is to be as creative as you can be. Injecting creativity into your lessons is a great way to put your stamp on the content you must cover. In addition, adding creativity reinforces having some personal control over what you are doing. Even if your lessons and curriculum are set in black and white by the principal, the school board or district, or even the state, try to find those elements that will add some pizzazz to what you are required to cover in class. Creative approaches to teaching material will excite your students, get their attention, and enhance their engagement and participation. Creativity can indeed make learning fun both for yourself and your students.

By showing your students how creativity is a viable tool in learning, you are modeling how they can use it for problem-solving in their own lives. Students need to learn to think outside the box, which can have powerful ramifications far into their future.

To convey this idea to the children I work with who may feel stuck and frustrated in dealing with a particular situation, I like to use stories of people who successfully used this tool. One of my favorites is the story of 18th-century British physician Edward Jenner. He had been trying to develop a treatment for the deadly disease smallpox at a time when its contagion rates were similar to the COVID virus, but had been unsuccessful. Frustrated by his inability to find an effective treatment or cure for this widespread disease, Jenner had a startling revelation – he realized that women who milked cows or worked in a dairy seemed to be immune to smallpox. Jenner hypothesized that these women developed an immunity to smallpox as a result of contracting the less severe disease cowpox through their work. Jenner believed there might be a connection between contracting cowpox and developing immunity to smallpox. He tested his theory by inoculating a child who had contracted smallpox with the cowpox virus, and the child's condition significantly improved. This led to widespread inoculation using the cowpox virus and the eventual eradication of smallpox. Jenner thought outside the box and tried a novel approach, resulting in countless lives saved all over the globe over the past 200 years!

Creativity has been defined as "the generation of a new product that's both novel and appropriate in a particular scenario. A product could be an idea, an artwork, an invention, or an assignment in your classroom."[13] This implies that there is no one single way to be creative. Indeed, many roads lead to Rome. By becoming an educator who is comfortable using creativity, you demonstrate that there can be great value in using innovative ideas. Questioning previously held notions, while unsettling initially, can lead to discoveries.

Utilizing creativity is also associated with developing intrinsic motivation, as previously discussed. The joy of the process can be incredibly exhilarating and liberating. Psychologist Robert Sternberg has pointed out that a student's level of creativity is even better at predicting success in college than a standardized test score.[14]

Becoming a strength-based teacher can include using healthy doses of creativity in your armamentarium or wheelhouse. Quite simply, creative teachers will foster the development of creativity in their students. Let students pick up on your playfulness, passion, and ability to bring concepts to life. When I was a teenager, I was a big fan of the television show *Welcome Back, Kotter* about a teacher who returns to the high school he attended to teach social studies. One of my favorite parts of the show was the way Mr. Kotter incorporated humor to bring material alive for his students. His impromptu skits illustrating American history were funny – and memorable.

Research cites the value of creativity for teachers and each of us. In one study, teachers kept a daily diary detailing their creative activities and tracking their emotions for nearly two weeks. Those participants who engaged in more creative activities experienced higher levels of positive emotions than those who did not participate in creative activities.[15] Teachers who take the time to engage in creative activities, whether playing a musical instrument or trying new recipes, can develop a positive mindset that will be passed on in their work with students. A study by IBM noted the value of creativity in leadership roles when managers recognized as creative were more effective in navigating challenges.[16] Finally, creativity has been associated with experiencing less anxiety, stress, and depression, as well as enhancing immune system functioning.[17]

A social studies teacher I know found a creative way to teach a required unit on countries around the world. She wrote the names of the countries to be covered on slips of paper, put them in a bowl and each student drew for their assignment. This allowed her to cover the required material while maintaining control over the process – students were not allowed to simply name a country they "liked," were already familiar with, or that was not challenging. After drawing the name of a country, the class was presented with a long list of activities to choose from to demonstrate their knowledge of some aspects about the country. These included:

♦ preparing a comprehensive report on the country;

♦ creating a word search or crossword puzzle with clues about the country for the class to fill out after the report;

♦ writing two tests for the class to take – one before and another after the report was presented;

♦ drawing maps for use in discussing the geography and climate of the country and how they have impacted the way people live; and another showing bordering countries, discussing the relationships between the two countries;

♦ reading a book about the country and writing a review of it;

♦ watching a movie that takes place in the country and reviewing it;

♦ performing a scene from that book or movie, or writing and performing an original skit about the country;

♦ explaining some of the country's customs;

♦ picking a famous person from the country and telling the class about them in a report or skit;

♦ telling the class about the native costumes of the people of the country – even dressing up as that person;

♦ relating a famous event that took place in the country;

♦ talking about famous people from the country and what they accomplished;

♦ Sharing music from the country – both from the past and the present; what do students in that country like to listen to; discuss composers and famous artists;

♦ showing photographs of famous buildings in the country like the Eiffel Tower, Big Ben, or the Leaning Tower of Pisa;

♦ telling about the sports that are played, including famous athletes and how the country has performed in the Olympics;

♦ discussing the country's role in the world. Is the United States on friendly terms with your country? If not, why not? Have we ever had a war with that country? Have we fought on the same side as allies?

♦ introducing the class to the country's food – do they like fish? Why do you think so? How do they like to prepare it? Discuss some recipes (even if you do not like them – sometimes the more exotic the dish, the more memorable the information will be to the class); where do they get the ingredients? Does a specific type of fruit grow there?

♦ describing what is it like to be poor in the country;

♦ discussing the religions practiced in the country; what are those practices like?

♦ talking about the culture of the country – what do they do there that is similar to things we do here in the United States? Do they Trick or Treat? Do they have something like the Super Bowl? What about Six Flags? What do they do that is entirely different from the United States?

♦ creating a model of a famous site in the country (for instance, the Eiffel Tower, The Matterhorn);

♦ creating a Lego scene or a clay model of a natural scene in the country.

Students were required to complete a minimum number of projects but allowed to take on as many as they wanted to earn the best grade they could. The students were enthusiastic and would often pick many activities beyond the minimum. The next year's students eagerly anticipated the "Countries Around the World" unit in this teacher's class as they had heard about it from older brothers and sisters and older students.

When we allow ourselves to be swept up in a state of creativity, our brainwaves slow down, making it easier to form original thoughts. Our prefrontal cortex will deactivate for a period, making us less self-critical. Neurotransmitters, such as dopamine, are released in such states, creating pleasurable emotions.[18]

There are additional ways for you to access your creativity.[19]

♦ Give some thought to your attitude toward creativity. Do you embrace it or feel uncomfortable going off script? Do you trust your instincts?

♦ Incorporate new methods to teach what you have been teaching the same way without change for years. Perhaps it can include a hands-on activity or other creative component, such as music, art, movies, plays, or skits.

♦ Listen to what your students are talking about. Did you happen to overhear them discuss a fad, a new toy, a video game, or song? Do some investigating to see if there is a way to incorporate these student interests into a lesson. For instance, a video game with a military theme can be related to a social studies lesson. One example is a very well-known video game, "The Oregon Trail®," that brings the era of western expansion in U.S. history alive for students as they outfit their Conestoga wagons and head across the prairie facing the dangers that the pioneers had to overcome.

♦ Find some time for yourself. While this may not always be easy, taking a break from our fast-paced, technology-filled world can be a great way to refresh and recharge creative juices.

♦ Switch up your daily routine. Find a different route to work (on purpose), listen to music you generally do not tune in to, read books on subjects or by authors you have no familiarity with, watch videos by artists you are not aware of, or incorporate new exercises in your workout. Activities such as these can help get you out of your rut and spur your creativity in other areas – like the classroom!

♦ Think about your hobbies and passions. Do they have a place in your lesson plans? Do you have a talent or skill you can use to teach material to your students?

♦ Do not be afraid of taking a risk and possibly failing. Be open to trying out new ideas and methods. Grow your teaching skills by infusing them with a dose (or two) of creativity.

◆ Do not be afraid of being creative, even if it may not come quickly. In her book, *Big Magic: Creative Living Beyond Fear*, author Elizabeth Gilbert asked, "Do you have the courage to bring forth the treasures that are hidden inside of you?"[20] This is a great question to promote self-examination and also one to ask our students.

Developing a Growth Mindset for Yourself

Sir Winston Churchill, British statesman, was known for his ability to state important concepts in a concise and witty manner as he did with this quote.

Attitude is a little thing that makes a big difference.[21]

Closely related to being creative is developing a growth mindset for yourself. As discussed earlier in relation to students, a growth mindset is characterized when you believe your abilities can be developed. Success depends on time and effort; talent and intellect are just regarded as starting points. Students with a growth mindset are not afraid of discovering their flaws. Indeed, they embrace them as a beginning from which they develop. In contrast, a fixed mindset is believing talent is all you need; making mistakes is experienced as highlighting your inadequacies.

Developing a growth mindset yields the same benefits for you as it does for your students. Doing so will help alleviate any pressure you may be putting on yourself to succeed unrealistically. It will help you become more creative and innovative in your teaching, rather than being afraid to deviate from what you know. Developing a growth mindset is also an invaluable way to model its benefits for your students, which will help them identify with and incorporate its value.

By not focusing primarily on students' grades nor being excessively concerned about making mistakes, but being more aware of the effort you put into your preparation and teaching, you will enhance the teaching and learning experience for yourself and your students. That kind of focus can also help you embrace challenging situations without feeling overwhelmed – a wonderful message to convey to your students in explicit and implicit ways.

When teachers have a predominantly fixed mindset, a potential problem for both the teachers and their students can occur, making it difficult for teachers to encourage their students to take academic risks. This can impede their ability to foster a growth mindset in their students.

Having a growth mindset may be a goal for most teachers, but how is it achieved? Here are some steps teachers can take to develop this critical perspective.

◆ Fight complacency. Do not come to believe you know all you need to know. Doing so can lead a teacher to reject or minimize the value of continued growth. A teacher with a growth mindset can be very proud of their skillset, but that does not mean they rest on their laurels! Far from it – they continue to seek new ideas, training, and additional learning opportunities.

◆ Become a lifelong learner. You can never be too old to learn something new. Just as we encourage our students to seek out new horizons academically, so must we. Take responsibility to improve your craft and increase your skillset by actively seeking new learning opportunities. As Mahatma Gandhi said, "Live as if you were to die tomorrow. Learn as if you were to live forever."[22]

◆ Innovate. Do not stay with the same lesson plans and teaching strategies simply because you have always relied on them. Instead, venture out of your comfort zone. Change things around. Investigate new methods to teach established ideas. There is no single way to teach. Vary the requirements of your assignments. Develop new assessments to use at the end of a unit. Show your students the value of thinking outside the box. "Innovation is progress in the face of tradition."[23]

♦ Do not be afraid to ask questions. Ask students, friends, family, and colleagues questions about how they learn. Ask your students what they would like to learn, what works for them in the classroom – and what does not. Ask yourself the same questions! Dig below the surface. Toddlers and young children learn by asking questions, which is their conduit to understanding the world around them. Then, as their understanding expands, students may become fearful of asking questions. Return to that time when you attempted to grasp novelty by getting to know it better. Encourage questions in the classroom and establish the attitude that there is no such thing as a "dumb" question – only the opportunity to learn. This is expressed by Sylvia Earle, research scientist and founder of Ocean Blue an organization dedicated to preserving the world's oceans:

The best scientists and explorers have the attributes of kids! They ask questions and have a sense of wonder. They have curiosity. "Who, what, where, why, when, and how!" They never stop asking questions, and I never stop asking questions, just like a five-year-old.[24]

♦ Flexibility is key. How can we teach students to change the world if we are reluctant to change our minds? The re-evaluation of ideas is crucial to a growth mindset. Learning to adapt to new information requires an open mind. Do not be afraid to adapt to new rules, stretch boundaries and take risks in attempting to reach your students.

♦ Do not be afraid of technology – embrace it! Chances are, your tech generation students are more well-versed in its intricacies than you are. Advances are constantly being made regarding educational programs, software, and methodologies. For example, before 2007, there was no such thing as an iPhone. Imagine if you turned your back on this and the subsequent technologies developed since then. You would have been missing out on a cultural revolution! You are in the business of teaching students new things every day. Why shouldn't that apply to you? You need not become an expert, but you will want to keep up with some of the more salient advances to see if these can be incorporated into your classroom.

◆ Listen! One of the main things we ask of our students is to do just that. Listening is more than hearing what the other person is saying. Taking in, processing, and absorbing what is heard is crucial to fostering a growth mindset. It may not be easy to consistently absorb the essence of what others are saying or avoid distractions, but by focusing on the messages we hear, a great deal of learning can occur. Do not rush to consider a response or to interject. Just take in what you are hearing.

◆ Reflect on what you are doing and how you are doing it. Self-evaluation is key to self-growth.

◆ Consider your strengths as well as any areas in which you feel challenged. Try to find the time to consider successes and disappointments and use them as an opportunity to learn about yourself. See setbacks and disappointments not as the end of the world but as the beginning of a new direction. Learn from these situations, take that knowledge, go forward with it and apply it where necessary. Experience it as an opportunity to improve your skills, not dwell on what you have not done well in the past.

Becoming a teacher who subscribes to a growth mindset perspective does not necessarily mean you explicitly teach your students the growth mindset qualities. Carol Dweck, the first to study this model, points out that rather than teaching students the exact points of having a growth mindset, instead take a nuanced approach and model the benefits by how you teach. Thus, it is not *telling them what to think* but instead *showing* students *how to think* that is important. Author Kate Herbert Smith wrote:

Growth mindset is about embodying it in all the everyday practices that educators do. Presenting material with students' understanding that you think they can all learn it to a high level. It's collaborating with students and giving feedback to them on their learning processes. It's about helping children to relish challenges because the challenges can help them grow their abilities.[25]

Handling Negative Feedback and Criticism

Robert Allen, author of several successful books on entrepreneurship offers this good advice,

There is no failure. Only feedback.[26]

While we constantly provide feedback to students, it is helpful to consider how to deal with feedback when we receive it. Teaching is a two-way street in terms of assessment. Even as you continuously evaluate students on several dimensions, it is fair to say that the same is happening to you, whether it is feedback from parents, administrators, colleagues, or the students themselves. When you choose to enter teaching, you run a high risk of multiple hits to your self-esteem. We need external support to help us through the storm, but that may not be enough. We must be able to cope with situations in which our esteem is threatened. Managing negative feedback from a strength-based perspective can be a helpful way to bolster your resilience.

Several years ago, I was a guest of a colleague teaching a course at a local college. At the end of the lecture, he told me that one of their students had decided to drop the class and informed the department chairperson that they were very disappointed by the quality of the teaching in his class. In contrast, none of the other students had dropped the course, and in prior years this colleague consistently received very positive feedback from students. Nevertheless, my friend was unhappy about that single student dropping the course. I tried to offer reassurance, but I knew my efforts would not alleviate his disappointment.

Why should my friend even experience that reaction? He fully understood that even one negative review could have a more significant impact than many positive reviews. However, this happens all the time in so many situations in life. Even though we know better, we let the negative outweigh the positive.

This phenomenon has been studied in psychology and is known as a negative bias. The origins of this particular bias go back to prehistoric times when cave dwellers had to be acutely attuned to any threats in their environment, be they human, animal, or from nature. Their very survival depended on this skill. Being hyperaware of possible threats enabled the species to survive.

Fast forward thousands of years. Fortunately for us, there are no wild animals on our streets, and for the most part, we can walk among others and not have to deal with a threatening situation. However, thousands of years of evolution have not undone the way our brains were initially wired. Humans are still hyper-sensitive to negativity in their environment. Despite the world being a very different place now, we are still poised to detect threats and negativity. As a result, we continue to exhibit negative bias.

I see this happening in many situations. A competent student who earns high grades reports feeling "devastated" after receiving a low, or even average, score on a test. Athletes who are highly consistent in their play get down on themselves when they cannot deliver in a tight situation. A professional who generally gathers praise for their efforts at work makes a mistake and rips themselves for it. In each situation, the focus was on the negative while "forgetting" many previously experienced positives. A single negative experience outweighed everything that had previously been accomplished.

In education, reviews and assessments are par for the course and can engender anxiety and dread for many. The fear of being critiqued looms large. This does not necessarily mean we are perfectionists who cannot tolerate falling short, although, for some, that may well be the case. For many of us in a modern-day world, our brains are wired in the same way they were eons ago. We continue to deal with this inborn tendency to accentuate the negative as a protective device to help ensure our survival in the face of threats – real or imagined.

As my friend found out in his class, in reality, you cannot please everyone. There is going to be blowback directed at you at some point. Even the Beatles, universally revered as one of the greatest, if not the greatest, band of all time, had to deal with a tremendous amount of rejection early in their career. However, despite the deep frustration and disappointment they must have felt, they were able to compartmentalize the rejection, avoid letting it overwhelm them, and continue to hone their craft. Eventually, they succeeded far beyond their wildest aspirations.

As a teacher, you may be exposed to many avenues of potential criticism – as well as possible praise. Administrators, parents, colleagues, and even students can potentially be messengers of bad tidings – sometimes valid, other times not. Dealing with this is a vital skill that should be developed. It is not just about developing a thick skin, although that helps. If you follow many of the tenets in this book, you will already have many skills to help you cope with negative feedback. Learning from mistakes, not forgetting the assets you bring to your role, and being kind to yourself are attributes of a strength-based teacher that can help you cope effectively with these situations.

In addition to relying on these qualities, there are other ways to deal with critical or negative feedback. Engage in self-care as soon as possible. Do rhythmic breathing after receiving negative feedback – right at that moment, if you can. Find a quiet spot and visualize relaxing or pleasant scenes from your life. It is not easy to process the feedback effectively until you feel calm.

While listening to the feedback:

◆ Do not get defensive. Let the person deliver it without interruption. Try to listen with an open mind, no matter how hard that may be.
◆ Do not react immediately. This will only frustrate the other party.
◆ Ask for concrete examples if the points seem confusing or vague.
◆ Do not personalize the feedback. The information you receive is limited to a particular part of your skillset. It does not negate the positive things you do. Try

compartmentalizing the feedback into a specific area rather than experiencing it as a blanket indictment of all aspects of your abilities or worth. Keep in mind that no matter how much you love your job, it does not define the totality of who you are.

◆ Avoid deflecting or ignoring the criticism or trying to justify your behavior. Doing so will only make you seem defensive.

◆ Do not attack the person offering the negative feedback even if they are unpleasant.

◆ In responding to the feedback, as painful as it may be, consider the possibility that there may be some truth to what you are hearing. Acknowledge any past mistakes and challenge yourself to do better in the future. Understand what contributed to the problem and actively try to change.

How we react to negative feedback can also help us become more sensitive when delivering it to our students. Tuning into our students' feelings allows us to give sensitive feedback while avoiding unnecessary hurt or emotional pain.

An exercise, such as focusing on what you love about teaching, can chase away negativity. Write down those things you do in the classroom that genuinely excite you about teaching and give you a feeling of absolute satisfaction. Brainstorm without censoring yourself. Even small things can be significant. Feel free to include anecdotes that illustrate the point you are listing. Keep a journal of those enriching events you experience to facilitate the process and explain why they brought you gratification; feel free to refer back to the list as needed. Refocus on what has made teaching special to you in the past – it can make you feel excited about teaching in the future.

Before falling asleep, I reflect on the day and recall anything I did that made at least one person happy. This has been highly challenging during the pandemic because, as a therapist, I see many people struggling with extreme, real-life circumstances. However, I try to come up with at least one thing I did that made a patient feel happier or more optimistic, and when I do, I hold onto that feeling and consider it a good day. Keeping this in mind helps me rekindle the excitement I feel about my role even in the face of challenges.

Focus on what makes you feel like singing and dancing about teaching. We work with real people. An intimidating responsibility indeed, but we get to see the outcome of our efforts in real-time. That is one of the great perks of teaching. I will never forget when I saw several children in succession, each of them presenting with exceedingly challenging life circumstances. It made me question what I could do to help them. Later that day, an eight-year-old child was telling me about a particularly upsetting incident. He suddenly stopped describing it and said,

> talking to you is like having a diary. Instead of writing it down, which I wouldn't do anyway unless the diary had a lock and key, I get to tell you about it. You are my lock and key, and I can feel I can tell you about it.

Hearing that invigorated me and helped me recall why I love my work.

Make a list of those aspects of your job you find the most gratifying. Think about incorporating them into your lesson plans or other classroom activities. At the same time, acknowledge possible constraints of reality and how these can impact your attempts to make your work more gratifying. Please do not give up; instead, find a way around your frustration with the situation. Think of it as going on a trip and discovering that the road is closed due to construction, forcing you to take a detour. The unplanned detour may be inconvenient and take longer but, eventually, you get to your destination. Along the way, you may discover new things to see that you might not have seen otherwise – beautiful scenery, an interesting monument, a new restaurant to try.

Look at all feedback, negative or positive, as a way to grow. Then, take that information and incorporate those aspects that make sense for your work.

The Importance of Self Care

Anne Lamott, author, offers these words of wisdom,

> Almost everything will work again if you unplug it for a
> few minutes, including yourself.[27]

The list of stressors unique to teaching is long. How many on this
list apply to you?

- having too many lessons to teach;
- modifying lessons for special needs students;
- devoting the appropriate amount of time to lesson
  preparation;
- addressing parental concerns;
- maintaining classroom discipline; and
- having excessive administrative work.

These stressors are solid and palpable. Teachers suffer from
among the highest levels of stress than any other profession,
with one in five teachers reporting feeling tense about their job
all or most of the time, compared with one in eight workers in
similar professions.[28] In one survey of midwestern elementary
school teachers, 93 percent reported high-stress levels. In the
study, teachers with low-stress levels and good coping skills
were practically nonexistent.[29] In a survey of over 500 teachers,
51 percent reported that the stress level is so high that they
have considered leaving the profession.[30] It is clear that teachers
who neglect their self-care place themselves at a higher risk for
burnout.

To be an effective strength-based educator, or to function
optimally in any role, self-care is essential. This cannot be
overemphasized. If you feel depleted, mentally and physically exhausted, overwhelmed, anxious or depressed, it will be
increasingly difficult to function in your classroom. In working
with families, I convey to parents the need to nurture themselves
to be the best possible parent. This is not being selfish – it is necessary. If there is no gas in the tank, the car will not go anywhere.

To cope with the stresses associated with teaching, it is crucial to stop and smell the roses along the way.

Speaking of flowers, a great way to start any conversation about self-care is to consider nature. As discussed earlier, spending time in nature is a potent (and free) way to reduce stress. The brain's prefrontal cortex, which plays a role in the rumination of negative thought, has lower activity levels when in nature and afterward. In addition, blood pressure can be lowered, and levels of the stress hormone cortisol are reduced. The more greenery we are exposed to, the less stress we experience.[31]

No time to go outdoors, or the weather is not inviting? No problem. Research indicates that watching nature videos or listening to recordings of the sounds of nature elevates our happiness levels and lowers our levels of depression and anxiety.[32] There are many channels online that feature hours of nature sounds, from gentle rain to thunderstorms, blizzards, forests, and beaches. These are great for meditation, falling asleep, or just as background sounds.

Another way to engage in self-care is to find time for what you feel passionate about. Whether through volunteering, reading, exercising, engaging in a hobby, music, art, binge-watching a television show, or becoming more faith-oriented, you need to have opportunities to allow your mind to relax and focus on yourself. Doing so has several benefits:

- ◆ experiencing a sense of personal freedom;
- ◆ feeling greater self-awareness and confidence as the more you are dedicated to your passion, the more you feel confident in overcoming challenges;
- ◆ enhancing a sense of purpose.

Recharging can not only improve your creativity[33,34] but can help improve your performance in the classroom.

Another excellent way to recharge your batteries is to engage in mindfulness activities, such as breathing exercises and mediation. The benefits of mindfulness on both our physical and mental well-being are well documented. These include being less likely to suffer from depression, anxiety, and stress while having higher happiness levels and improved memory, concentration, and focus. Physically, mindfulness stimulates a more robust immune system and reduces physical pain. It also helps promote more satisfying interpersonal relationships and higher job performance rates. With the availability of online programs, it has never been more convenient to engage in these activities.

A mindfulness training program geared specifically for teachers has been developed by Christa Turksma, who formed the Cultivating Awareness and Resilience for Educators (CARE) program,[35,36] and runs summer retreats to teach the principles of mindfulness to educators. Participants reported a significant decrease in anxiety, depression, burnout, and overall stress following the retreat.

Turksma has also studied the impact of CARE training on New York City teachers. When they returned to their classrooms, teachers experienced more significant levels of engagement with students than in the past and reported that they raised their voices much less frequently. The teachers also said their classes were more emotionally positive and productive than before they learned about mindfulness.

Stressful teachers create stressful students. In a recent study, students had higher levels of the neurotransmitter cortisol associated with stress in classrooms where teachers admitted to suffering from burnout.[37]

In another study, researchers found that when teachers are highly stressed, it often leads to lower academic performance and less adequate social adjustment for their students. In this same study, it was noted that teachers who had high levels of stress were at greater risk for physical and mental health difficulties, sleep problems, poor work performance, and higher absenteeism rates.[38] Think about how presenting yourself as stressed, irritable, and mentally exhausted will impact your ability to do your job.

Keep in mind that educators are vulnerable to several hits to their self-esteem potentially daily from various sources. Without support externally and internally, you can risk becoming burned out and relating to students in a punitive manner. So ... find that time to unplug, unwind, and feel unencumbered by life's demands. It is an investment in yourself that will pay dividends, invigorate your work in the classroom, and benefit your students. As the author Eleanor Brown states, "Rest and self-care are so important. When you take time to replenish your spirit, it allows you to serve others from the overflow. You cannot serve from an empty vessel."[39]

Foster Relationships at Work

Communication expert and author Michelle Tillis Lederman states,

> Whether they stem from business or personal situations, our relationships are what support us, connect us, and allow us to progress in all aspects of our lives.[40]

Establishing positive relationships with your peers is indispensable in achieving resilience at work. In my case, I can unequivocally say that the friendships I cultivated at work were critical in helping me deal with challenges. My colleagues served a variety of roles. These ranged from being valued team members whose insights added to my understanding of the students we worked with, to friends. In addition to just being fun to hang out with and sharing each other's company, these relationships truly helped enhance my work experience. Having that solid supportive network made me feel more confident in situations that required some degree of risk, and my close work friendships allowed me to challenge myself in ways I probably would not have otherwise.

Supportive relationships enhance our day-to-day lives and contribute to longevity.[41] Working in an encouraging environment with people you trust and genuinely enjoy can fulfill the work experience, so do not avoid the teacher's lounge. Chat up your colleagues. Collectively, they can be an excellent source of inspiration, advice, and support. Employees who reported that they had a best friend at work felt more engaged at their job.[42] Good buddies at work are more than just people to sit with at lunch – they strengthen our identification with the organization we work for and enhance our health and well-being.[43] The greater our social identification with colleagues, the more we accrue physical and psychological benefits regardless of career path. Higher levels of organizational commitment, job satisfaction, and overall positive emotions were reported by teachers who experienced their peers as compassionate.

Teaching is a relationship business. Forging relationships with students, parents, colleagues, and administrators is part of what we do. We can tap into a wonderful source of empathy and understanding by not neglecting that group of people in the trenches with us who can most readily relate to what we are doing. Teachers who report positive connections with their colleagues enjoy the following benefits:[44]

♦ They believe their coworkers are not only friendly but also care about them.
♦ They experience a significant level of respect and trust in each other.
♦ They see each other as accepting, encouraging, collaborative, and supportive.
♦ They feel they can communicate openly with colleagues and go to them for help.

Other benefits of positive work relationships in schools include those listed below:[45,46]

♦ Student teachers who felt the staff got along well were more likely to want to work at that school.
♦ Teachers feel more committed to teaching when they have support from their peers and administrators.
♦ Teachers work more collaboratively when they trust each other.
♦ Research in urban high schools shows that positive staff relations lead to a better school climate, which, in turn, contributes to students' academic achievement.

◆ Similarly, collegial behavior between staff is essential for distinguishing high-performing from low-performing middle schools.

Make an effort to get to know your colleagues by cultivating a genuine interest in them. Ask about their backstory, their families, and hobbies. Doing this gradually will allow you to determine if you want to know this person. This can lay the foundation for a real friendship. Offer to help if you see a colleague struggling. This will go a long way toward forging a positive connection.

Consider joining committees or working on projects with other teachers. This is a great way to step outside your work bubble and know your colleagues better. As an added benefit, you will learn about different facets of how your school or district operates.

Be positive. Have a sunny disposition. No one will want to know you if you do not seem approachable. Do not habitually complain about work. That can be a huge turnoff.

Do not make it all about you. Revealing too much personal information too soon can make people question your judgment. This is particularly true in work settings. Let your friendships at work develop naturally over time before sharing personal life details.

Do not be an island unto yourself at school.

Subscribing to a strength-based model focuses on tapping into your students' resources and emphasizes doing the same for yourself. The ideas presented in this chapter can help pave the way for that. To give to others, we must have the resources available within ourselves to share. This is not selfish but rather a way to provide growth-enhancing experiences for your students. The methods described in this chapter – getting in touch with your story of origin, focusing on what inspired you to teach in the first place and your desire to teach well, dealing only with things you can control as well as being creative, handling negative feedback, paying attention to self-care, and reaching out to colleagues will go a long way to sustaining you in your quest to be a strength-based teacher for your students and building a rewarding career in the classroom.

References

1. Scholar, J. (2018, April, 30) "Miss L's third grade thoughts." Blog. https://publish.illinois.edu/uistudteachaml/2018/04/
2. Kalam, A. (2022). "A.P.J. Abdul Kalam Quotes." *BrainyQuote* www.brainyquote.com/quotes/a_p_j_abdul_kalam_717997
3. Study International Staff. (2019, June 10). "Teachers are more depressed and anxious than the average Australian." www.studyinternational.com/news/teachers-are-more-depressed-and-anxious-than-the-average-australian/
4. Schaffauser, D. (2020, June 2). "Educators feeling stressed, anxious, overwhelmed, and capable." https://thejournal.com/articles/2020/06/02/survey-teachers-feeling-stressed-anxious-overwhelmed-and-capable.aspx
5. Looking Back Quotes. No date. AZ *Quotes*. www.azquotes.com/quotes/topics/looking-back.html
6. Merriam-Webster. (2022). Website www.merriam-webster.com/dictionary/origin
7. "Marcus Aurelius Quotes." (2022). *Goodreads* www.goodreads.com/quotes/190580-you-have-power-over-your-mind-not-outside-events
8. Brooks, R. (2003, February 14). "Further thoughts about personal control." Website. www.drrobertbrooks.com/0302/
9. Ibid.
10. Ibid.
11. Ibid.
12. Robinson, K. (2007, January 7). "Do schools kill creativity?" Ted Talk. https://youtu.be/iG9CE55wbtY
13. Davis, L. (2018, December 17). "Creative teaching and teaching creativity: How to foster creativity in the classroom." http://psychlearningcurve.org/creative-teaching-and-teaching-creativity-how-to-foster-creativity-in-the-classroom/
14. Ibid.
15. Conner T., DeYoung, C., & Silvia, P. (2018) "Everyday creative activity as a path to flourishing." *The Journal of Positive Psychology*, 13(2), 181–189, doi: 10.1080/17439760.2016.1257049
16. Martin, C. & Hedges, K. (2010, July 16). "Creativity is the new black." www.forbes.com/sites/work-in-progress/2010/07/16/creativity-is-the-new-black/?sh=7999908f62df

17. Brenner, B. (2019, September 16). "Creativity is your secret advantage for mental health and well-being." yctherapy.com/therapists-nyc-blog/creativity-is-your-secret-advantage-for-mental-health-and-well-being/

18. https://nyctherapy.com/therapists-nyc-blog/creativity-is-your-secret-advantage-for-mental-health-and-well-being/

19. Davis, L. (2018, December 17). "Creative teaching and teaching creativity: How to foster creativity in the classroom." http://psychlearningcurve.org/creative-teaching-and-teaching-creativity-how-to-foster-creativity-in-the-classroom/

20. Gilbert, E. (2015). *Big Magic: Creative Living Beyond Fear.* Riverhead Books.

21. "Winston Churchill Quotes." (2022*). BrainyQuote.* www.brainyquote.com/quotes/winston_churchill_104164

22. "10 Power quotes that inspire you to never stop learning." *Inspiration Unlimited Magazine* (January, 2017) www.iuemag.com/january2017/di/10-power-quotes-never-stop-learning.php

23. James, A. No date. "Innovation is progress in the face of tradition." Post on LinkedIn. www.linkedin.com/posts/ajjames_innovation-is-progress-in-the-face-of-tradition-activity-6858174767120314368-N3Xn/

24. Nest, S. (2022) "36 Quotes from successful people about the wisdom in asking questions." *Lifehack.* www.lifehack.org/articles/productivity/36-quotes-from-successful-people-about-the-wisdom-asking-questions.html

25. Herbert-Smith, K. (2018, March 29). "Growth mindset: The key to successful teaching?" Post on Blog Iris Connect. https://blog.irisconnect.com/uk/community/blog/5-attributes-of-a-growth-mindset-teacher/

26. Allen, R. (2015, June 28). https://doncharisma.org/2015/06/28/there-is-no-failure-only-feedback/

27. Timms, E. (2019, February 18). "Healthy work environment: How to create your own." *Healthy* Balance. University Of Virginia Health. https://blog.uvahealth.com/2019/02/18/healthy-work-environment/

28. Busby, E. (2019, September 22). "Teachers suffer more stress than other workers, study finds." Blog The American Institute of Stress. www.stress.org/teachers-suffer-more-stress-than-other-workers-study-finds

29. Herman, K., Reinke, W., & Hickmon-Rosa. J. (2018). "Empirically derived profiles of teacher stress, burnout, self-efficacy, and coping and associated student outcomes." *Journal of Positive Behavior Interventions*, 20(2), 90–100.

30. Hess, A. (2019, August 9). "50% of teachers surveyed say they've considered quitting, blaming pay, stress, and lack of respect." CNBC. www.cnbc.com/2019/08/09/50percent-of-teachers-surveyed-say-theyve-considered-quitting-teaching.html

31. Sreekanth, A. (2017, March 20). "UC Berkeley study reveals watching nature videos can increase happiness." *The Daily Californian*. www.dailycal.org/2017/03/20/uc-berkeley-study-reveals-watching-nat ure-videos-can-increase-happpiness/

32. Ibid.

33. Stillman, J. (2019, October 14). "5 incredible, research-backed benefits of having a passion outside work." *Inc.* /jessica-stillman/5-incredible-research-backed-benefits-of-having-a-passion-outside-work.html

34. Stillman, J. (2014, May 6). "How your hobbies impact your work performance." *Inc.* www.inc.com/jessica-stillman/how-your-hobb ies-effect-work-performance.html

35. Kamentz, A. (2016, August 19). "Why teachers say practicing mindfulness is transforming the work." *Mindshift*. www.kqed.org/mindsh ift/46150/why-teachers-say-practicing-mindfulness-is-transform ing-the-work

36. CARE for Teachers Program. Website. https://hundred.org/en/inno vations/care-cultivating-awareness-and-resilience-in-education-for-teachers#d7069609

37. "Top 3 Causes of Teacher Stress and How it Affects Students." (2018, May, 23). *Learning Liftoff* www.learningliftoff.com/how-teacher-str ess-affects-students/

38. Berrett, S. (2021, April 21). "How physical stress impacts you and your classroom." *Eschool News*. www.eschoolnews.com/2021/04/ 21/how-physical-stress-impacts-you-and-your-classroom/2/

39. Sobelson, B. & Hyde H. (2017, December 8). "Caring for yourself and others: 7 tips for the holiday season." *Military Families Learning Network*. https://militaryfamilieslearningnetwork.org/2017/12/08/ caring-for-yourself-and-others-7-tips-for-caregivers-during-the-holiday-season/

40. "Famous quotes about building oneself." (2022). *Insight*. https://quotesinsight.com/topic/building-oneself-quotes/

41. Evans, K. (2018, September 17). "Why relationships are the key to longevity." *Mindful*. www.mindful.org/why-relationships-are-the-key-to-longevity/

42. Kaado, B. (2022, August 5). "Why it's good to have a BFF at work." *Business Work Daily*. www.businessnewsdaily.com/6759-friends-at-work.html

43. Malacoff, J. (2016, November 28). "Here's why it's important to get along with your coworkers." *Glassdoor*. www.glassdoor.com/blog/heres-why-its-important-to-get-along-with-your-coworkers/

44. "Positive staff relationships." (2022). *Greater Good in Education*. https://ggie.berkeley.edu/school-relationships/positive-staff-relationships/#tab__2

45. Pride Surveys. (2016, July 15). www.pridesurveys.com/index.php/blog/4-beneficial-effects-of-student-teacher-relationships/

46. "The Importance of Strong Relationships." (2021, May 17). *The Education Trust*. https://edtrust.org/resource/the-importance-of-strong-relationships/

7

Implications for the Future: Where Do We Go from Here?

One of the leading 20th-century voices in psychology and parenting was Dr. Haim Ginott. It is almost impossible to overstate his contribution to education. His words about the power a teacher has in the classroom still ring true today.

> I've come to a frightening conclusion that I am the decisive element in the classroom. It's my personal approach that creates the climate. It's my daily mood that makes the weather. As a teacher, I possess a tremendous power to make a child's life miserable or joyous. I can be a tool of torture or an instrument of inspiration. I can humiliate or heal. In all situations, it is my response that decides whether a crisis will be escalated or de-escalated and a child humanized or dehumanized.[1]

The Need for a Strength-Based Culture in Schools

A strength-based approach is far more than applying rote strategies in the classroom. It builds a culture that places a premium on student engagement, enhancing resilience and success. The beauty of this model is that it is not reserved just for particular

DOI: 10.4324/9781003368014-8

segments of the student population but is available for use with students across the gamut, whether learning disabled, on the autism spectrum, in a gifted program, or a mainstream class. All students can benefit from what this perspective offers. Moreover, the model emphasizes that children hold the key to transforming themselves into the best version of who they can be.

As I write this, we are well into the third year of the COVID pandemic with an easing of some restrictions while we develop therapeutics and await possible new variants, making it endemic rather than a pandemic. I have significant concerns about how children – and the rest of us – will transition to whatever the "new normal" may be. Many of us will not need any encouragement to rip off our masks and head to our favorite restaurant, take in a concert or attend a football game while mingling with friends and strangers. However, it is fair to say that not everyone will be eager or even ready to go charging back into the world. Many will have a difficult time assimilating to the new reality. They will fret over how to resume some semblance of the regular familiar social interactions we were accustomed to before the pandemic. It has been drummed into our brains to wear masks, maintain social distance, and refrain from being part of large groups. For those children who have been isolated, with the bulk of their social interaction coming via a screen, how they will react to resuming some semblance of in-person interaction poses a question worthy of consideration.

While many of the children I have seen in therapy during the pandemic had difficulty adapting to the new reality, many students did well and flourished. Freed from the demands of attending school and being placed in social situations that were previously anxiety-ridden or even terrifying for them, these children, who already had high levels of social anxiety, quickly adapted to remote schooling. One such adolescent with significant social anxiety told me when I asked him how he was feeling, "I'm doing great! I have been social distancing for years!" How will this youth, along with countless others, adapt to returning to life – or some new version of it – as it used to be?

Fostering a strength-based culture in schools will be extremely helpful for these particular students as they return to school. A culture promoting resilience and emotional grit is essential as students adapt to a world that may be incredibly challenging for them. Students will need tools to cope as they return to school and move into higher education, jobs, or the military in the changed post-pandemic world. They will need to be able to tap into their assets in ways they never had to do previously. Teachers are "first responders" in this quest.

Forming a Strength-Based Culture in Schools

Developing a strength-based culture in a school is not an easy task. While the benefits are impressive, merely wanting to establish such a culture does not automatically translate into achieving that result; a few impediments must be addressed.

First is to acknowledge that change creates anxiety, and one way people cope with uncertainty is to avoid the thing that makes them uncomfortable and want to cling, sometimes tenaciously, to the familiar. This will occur even if they understand that holding onto old patterns or ideas may not be totally in their best interest.

Second, some educators may view the strength-based perspective as artificially pumping students up by showering them with false praise or exaggerated platitudes. For many, addressing a child's deficits is the preferred way to assist them, while adherence to a strength-based model may be seen as ignoring a child's weaknesses to their detriment. This reveals a basic misunderstanding of the nature of strength-based teaching, the belief in remediating problems by solely addressing weaknesses will undermine attempts to use a strength-based approach.

Third, teacher training would need to be modified to incorporate strength-based teaching, relationship-building principles, and strategies into the curriculum. Teachers need to be immersed in this perspective during their training in order for it to become second nature. This process can be time-consuming and expensive, as remedial programs require teachers' time reading materials on the strength-based model and attending training sessions. Mentors and trainers versed in this model will require resources to share it with school staff. However, the costs of not taking these necessary steps may be much higher in the long run. Diversifying the allocation of existing resources can help address this issue.

Fourth, enhancing resilience and fostering productive teacher/student relationships, while sounding like good ideas, often take a back seat to the role of assessment. If teachers feel they will be judged mainly by their students' performance on standardized measures, it is only natural that many of them will prioritize student success on these tests. This will place teacher/student relationships and student resilience on the back burner in favor of "teaching to the test."

Any change or growth in an organization starts with a basic premise: Will the potential audience buy into what is being presented? I have been in many professional development classes where well-meaning presenters put forth various ideas only to be met with disinterest, skepticism, or even resistance by the audience. Thought must be given to how to present the concept and strategies to promote some degree of receptivity amongst the audience, in this case, teachers and administrators.

Teachers and administrators need greater clarity on the perspective of strength-based teaching. This can be achieved when the model of strength-based culture, its foundation, and basic premises are presented, which will build confidence and interest in introducing the concept into the learning environment.

The strength-based model relies on some basic assumptions.[2]

- ◆ Every student has potential. This must be a firmly held foundational belief as it is the bedrock of all other ideas. Can teachers and administrators accept that each student's unique collection of strengths and capabilities will eventually come to write their developing story and define who they are rather than who they are not?
- ◆ What we choose to focus on will become a student's reality. Thus, a strength-based view will focus on what students *can* do rather than what they *cannot*. Challenges

are viewed as opportunities to explore rather than situations to avoid, starting with small successes and gradually building upon them to promote hope and optimism.

◆ Knowing that our words impact our students. There is a big difference between telling a student, "Didn't you hear what I told the other students?" and "It looks like you tried doing this exercise another way; let us see how that worked for you."

◆ Imposing ideas and beliefs upon students that are not consistent with the student's perceptions and ideas are doomed to fail. Any intervention takes as its starting point where the student is and respects that perspective. Teachers must be sensitive to this. If a student has a negative self-perception and you tell them they have fantastic potential, they may tune you out. An excellent first step is to empathize and validate how the student is feeling. Try to normalize how the student is feeling. For instance, say, "It's hard to get work done when you are tired ... I also have days when I make mistakes ... yes, that is hard."

◆ School staff members need to accept that all students desire to succeed and can grow. Positive change for students can best be facilitated when they recognize that the adults in their school genuinely care about them, want them to succeed, and are available for support when needed. Above all, genuine relationships are key. This premise, above all others, is the most critical in fostering a strength-based mindset.

These ideas form the basis for a strength-based culture in schools. It is not enough to articulate them and leave it at that – the staff needs to see the value of these beliefs in guiding student behaviors, as well as their own. Further, the culture of the school needs to reflect these ideas. All school staff members need to adhere to these principles in their dealings with students. Interactions with students must be done in a way that communicates positive attitudes about the student's dignity and capabilities while at the same time drawing upon the student's strengths to achieve progress toward their goals.

Educators do not need to choose between academic success and emotional well-being; a strength-based culture adheres to the belief that the two are intertwined. Academic success can more readily occur when teachers communicate their belief in a student's potential while allowing students to explore, understand, and have opportunities to utilize their strengths. Without this element, students will not be primed to achieve. As psychologist Shawn Achor notes, "Positive brains are not only our best defense against negativity, stress, and challenge, they are the best source of the adaptability, creativity, and innovation needed to address the problems we face and mountains we intend to climb."[3]

To help teachers grasp the value of the strength-based approach, school administrators need to promote an atmosphere where the positive is always accentuated, and seeing the glass as always half-full is accepted as the norm. Anything less than that will undermine the strength-based culture and prevent it from taking hold. Further, teachers must also be provided with the practical resources needed to implement and foster such a culture, including commercially available workbooks that provide strength-based exercises, as well as arts and crafts materials for students to showcase their abilities. Teachers need support to implement the strength-based model in the classroom. This can be achieved through collaborating and brainstorming with their colleagues.

Such collaboration can occur after classroom or subject assignments are set for the upcoming school year. The teacher who has been working with a student during the current year can meet with the teacher who will have the student in their class the following school year to review the student's strengths and those learning strategies that worked best for them. In this way, the following year's teacher will have valuable information to apply at the start of the new year to best utilize the capabilities of the student. Resilience-building strategies should be shared between teachers and passed on from one grade to the next. It is also helpful to keep in mind that the teacher does not want to pick up any negative impression of a student they will have in the next class. Acquiring a negative bias against a student based on another teacher's experience or opinion can prevent a teacher from applying strength-based strategies in the new year. It should always be considered that every new academic year provides students with the opportunity of a fresh start – give them the benefit of a clean slate when they walk in your door in September.

While the teacher/student relationship is crucial to fostering a strength-based classroom, teachers also need to have supportive relationships with their administrators. Just as students need teachers to trust them and believe in what they can do, teachers need similar support from the school and district administrations.

In fostering a strength-based approach in your school, you and your colleagues need to ask yourselves some essential questions.

◆ Do I provide care and support to the student? Do my words and actions convey that I genuinely care about them?

◆ Do I set and clearly communicate high expectations for my students?

◆ Do I believe all students can succeed? Do I provide the necessary support for them to do so?

◆ Do I address different learning styles in my lessons? Am I flexible in accommodating different personalities and learning styles? Do I provide students with an opportunity to show me what they do well?

◆ Do I provide opportunities for students to participate in meaningful ways?

◆ Do I allow students to take on different roles and responsibilities?

◆ Do I offer students the chance to bond with their peers? Do I connect students in ways that help them get to know one another?

◆ Do I show respect to students and colleagues and expect it from others?

◆ Do I model courtesy and politeness and expect it from my students?

◆ Do I set clear and consistent boundaries in the classroom? Are logical consequences for failure to observe the boundaries expressed consistently and applied fairly?

♦ Am I teaching life skills that help students make decisions and resolve conflicts? Do my students have opportunities to practice making decisions?

♦ Can they choose from a variety of engaging projects? Are there options for them to demonstrate their knowledge? Do I provide opportunities for them to work together and have experiences as a team member?

The following ideas can stimulate your thinking about how you, your colleagues, your school, and your district can enhance your relationships with students and utilize their assets. They are based in part on the work of the Alberta Mentoring Program to create strength-based classrooms.[4] We will next look at how this can occur within the classroom, school, and at district levels.

Teacher Level Approaches

Students need to know you value them. Treating students in a kind, respectful manner goes a long way to developing and maintaining a trusting relationship. A teacher I worked with would stand by the classroom door as the students entered, say good morning, and address them by their first name. In addition to setting a positive tone for the day, this is one way to let students know you value them. When students feel they matter to you, it does wonders for their esteem and contributes to more engaged learners. It is also a beneficial tool to help buffer your students from anxiety and depression.

An additional side effect of this approach is that happier children usually lead to peaceful and productive classrooms. Modeling kindness for your students promotes empathic behavior. Students can become more adept at recognizing how others feel, making for stronger relationships. Make it a priority to plant the seeds of positive social behavior for your students. Those lessons and their impact can last for their entire lifetimes.

Help students feel connected to their school. Students need to become active members of the school community to form a sense of school identification. School can be a place to try out additional roles beyond their primary one as a student by encouraging the student to participate in ways designed to showcase their interests and strengths. I remember a fifth-grade boy who struggled academically and had behavioral outbursts. He was, however, a wiz at technology. His teacher and I came up with the idea of him being the "tech guy" for his class who would help run selected school events that relied on technology. We helped him find an opportunity to step out of the frustration he experienced and use his competencies. He enjoyed his role tremendously and never let us down.

Try to think of ways your students can connect to their school and bring something meaningful to the table. In addition to helping out in the classroom, suggest they serve as peer tutors assisting younger students or those with special needs – a strategy I saw utilized many times and often with impressive results for everyone involved. Perhaps they can serve on committees to help your school meet specific goals. Organize student fundraisers. Decorate the common areas for special events. Encourage students to participate in extracurricular clubs, teams, and activities to foster a stronger connection. This can also help develop a greater school identity.

Students who feel that they do not "belong" to their school are at risk for anxiety, depression, and loneliness. It is not an exaggeration to say that how strongly students feel they belong will have long-term ramifications on their emotional well-being well into adulthood. Students who lack a bond with their school can experience a negative impact on their academic functioning – another long-lasting negative impact.

One of the most potent ways to create a cohesive school culture and promote student resiliency is to provide students with relationships they can rely on. It is no overstatement to say that a caring relationship with students is one of the most important, if not the essential, things you can provide for them. This point has been repeatedly raised throughout this book as it is the foundation for quality learning in the classroom. As stated in an earlier chapter, students will not care unless they think you do – it all comes down to that. I have heard so many students from elementary school through high school voice how turned off they are to school, and in most instances, it comes down to a lack of a trusting relationship with a teacher or counselor.

Keep the following ideas in mind while building relationships with your students. Be very aware of your biases. We are all the products of our experiences, so what may seem familiar and ordinary to us may be totally out of the realm of your students' experience due to socio-cultural factors, location, ethnicity, and, certainly, age. Take the time to get to know your students' life experiences and their reactions to them. Being aware of a student's home environment can help you better understand their needs and life outside school. Talk to them about their families, interests, and hobbies. This can be invaluable information to incorporate into your lessons to meet your students' needs more effectively. In doing so, however, make sure you adhere to professional boundaries.

Do not hold a grudge. It is natural to feel angry with a student if they misbehave, and that feeling may be difficult to shake. Ultimately this is counterproductive. Each of us can have a bad day. We are not privy to students' circumstances before and after school, at home, and within their families, on the playground, in other classes, on the football field or basketball court. I am not advocating letting students off the hook for inappropriate behavior; each of us needs to take ownership of the consequences of our actions. However, to truly build a relationship based on trust and respect, every day needs to be treated as a new one that offers students a fresh start.

In communicating with students, staff members need to remember that the best way to convey support is to listen, validate the student's feelings, and demonstrate compassion and respect. Most students are doing the best they can, shaped by their prior experiences, current situation, and how they perceive their world. Your caring relationship with a student may be the only area in their life that fuels hope and optimism for them.

Most relevant to this discussion is a study in which students of various ages were shown videotapes of teachers talking about or with students for whom they had high or low expectations.[5] The respondents noted clear and consistent differences in how the teachers spoke about their students. The students watching the videos were asked to rate the teacher based on various characteristics. The student sample watching the video could tell rather quickly if the teacher liked the student and expected them to succeed. The student sample rated the highly regarded student discussed by the teacher in the video more positively than those students the teachers did not speak of highly. While we are watching our students, they are assessing us as well.

As mentioned earlier, connecting with students must precede teaching. Only when this groundwork is laid will you and your students be able to embark on the most incredible journey of learning together. As a school principal once said to his faculty at a meeting, "For whom are you going to work harder ... someone you like or someone you do not like?"[6]

Go out of your way to celebrate a student's success, no matter its size. I recall a teenager who wanted to audition for the school play but was overcome by anxiety and chose not to take the risk. Instead, the student worked on the stage crew behind the scenes. When his senior year arrived and with it, the final chance to audition for a role, he steeled himself and tried out. He passed the audition, not only winning a singing part, but also earning a small solo. That this anxious teen could get past his fear of auditioning was huge – winning the solo was a bonus. The student never forgot this achievement – it promoted feelings of accomplishment and competence that could be drawn upon when needed in future situations.

Challenge your students to be the best possible version of themselves and share your confidence in their ability to achieve that goal.

While competition may be fun on the athletic field, it can adversely affect the classroom. A highly competitive classroom can instill fear and anxiety in students. It can lead students to worry if they will measure up to what they think parents and teachers expect. In one study, students were assigned a task and randomly placed in either a competitive or non-competitive situation. Students in the competitive group were less likely to take risks if they believed they could not achieve a positive outcome, thus limiting their learning opportunities. They were also more likely to have a negative self-evaluation after failing.[7]

In contrast, a strength-based classroom promotes a culture of cooperation. This is an atmosphere where students can feel safe, secure, and eager to learn. The goal is not to compare themselves to their peers but rather to recognize their efforts and foster greater bonding. Students can pay more attention to the learning process than the outcome when they do not compare themselves to others. Complimenting your students' individual and group efforts goes a long way to promoting a cooperative classroom. This atmosphere motivates students to play a more significant role in setting goals. This can also help them encourage each other to learn.

Have positive expectations and keep them high. Students benefit from a structure that helps offer them an understanding of goals to strive for. An open-ended set of vague and diffuse expectations can lead to students being confused and frustrated. Students work best when they know what is expected of them. Having high expectations for students conveys that you want to help them do their best and that you firmly believe they are capable of doing perhaps even more than they think they can do. Inspire your students to dream by encouraging them to persevere. Of course, goals may need to be tempered so keep them realistic. Having clear expectations for your students will allow them to direct their efforts realistically while enhancing their chances of success. Teacher expectations can become a self-fulfilling prophecy. Children have a sense of what they believe they can do, and our expectations go a long way toward fueling a student's beliefs about what they can or cannot achieve. Encourage stretching by setting realistic goals that can be met, then helping students set new, more challenging goals to establish a pattern of trying and succeeding.

Having high expectations of your students is not intended to frustrate them or serve as a justification to ride them to the limits of their endurance. Instead, it conveys your belief that they can do more, and you will not accept anything less than their best effort. A task may have to be redone or reconfigured along the way, but it can be an opportunity for you to help them learn perseverance.

This holds true even for those students who present with learning challenges. If necessary, utilize alternative methods and strategies to meet students' needs. Be as inventive as you can. Perhaps have them teach younger students content they have mastered; this can help boost their confidence. If a student has written language difficulties, offering alternatives to express what they know, such as reciting their work orally, can help them demonstrate mastery of content.

Dr. Carol Dweck's work on mindsets notes that when a teacher's mindset about a student's ability is fixed, meaning, in the words of the great comedian Flip Wilson, "what you see is what you get," the student will not disappoint. If you have a fixed negative mindset, the student will be more likely to live up – or down – to our low expectations. The student's level of achievement will not significantly increase over the school year. Students with teachers who believe they can grow will do so more readily than students who do not receive the benefits from teachers who believe in them.[8] To set high expectations for your students requires keeping several points in mind.

- ◆ Convey confidence in your students.
- ◆ Allow students to contribute and voice their opinions.
- ◆ Provide specific, individualized feedback as opposed to vague, general feedback.
- ◆ Provide your students with work content that is neither easy nor too difficult for them to complete, or that would frustrate them. In other words, give them content that is just right for their ability level. You want to stimulate their desire to learn while not disheartening them.

Search out a child's strengths sooner than later. When I first meet a youngster referred to me for psychotherapy, I ask them what they are good at and do well. This question may often throw the child as they may have at least a vague idea that they will be meeting with me due to some difficulties in their lives. So, a question like this is often unexpected.

Often, a child will respond that they do not know of anything they can do well. Even when I try to prod for an answer, many children will continue to assert that they have no unique capabilities. In that case, I will respond that sometimes it can be hard to think of one, but we will figure that out as we get to know each other.

Children who are not aware of their strengths may feel hopeless about themselves and their future. They do not envision how these feelings can impact their lives in any meaningful way and approach new tasks with a sense of resignation and helplessness, convinced that they will not do well.

Helping a child discover signature strengths can be one of the most powerful things you can do for them. Just as teacher perceptions impact how successful a student will be, they are also helpful in shaping a child's self-view. It can open their eyes to new worlds around them, helping them genuinely to see themselves in a new light, often for the first time in their life.

The amount of time we spend with students can exceed children's time with their parents. Public school teachers are in the classroom an average of 1001 hours per year at the pre-primary level, 782 hours at the primary level, 694 hours at the lower secondary level, and 655 hours at the upper secondary level.[9] That is an incredible amount of time spent with a child teaching and influencing them in an average school year of nine to ten months. In contrast, a recent study concluded that, on average, parents spend five hours per week in face-to-face time with their children – a far less amount of time than teachers.[10] Teachers are uniquely positioned to positively influence children, perhaps even to a greater extent than parents.

Emotional education is a big part of what teachers do. For instance, showing children how to demonstrate persistence even in the face of ongoing adversity is another gift you can offer students that will pay dividends over their lifetime. Just watching how you manage challenges in the classroom, reassure a student who may be struggling, or share personal anecdotes that illustrate perseverance can communicate this quality very effectively.

Explain to your students that emotions are universal to us all, and our feelings will often impact how we learn and solve problems. Emotions are not something to deny or suppress – we need to acknowledge them, and if that does not help, we figure out ways to cope with them. Students need to understand that emotions allow them to persevere and should not be feared even though they may be confusing and uncomfortable – even scary, at times.

A beneficial strategy is to remind students to prepare for commonplace obstacles by having a backup or "Plan B." One analogy that Charles Appelstein, a well-known strengths-based therapist, uses is to tell children to imagine they are heading to a destination. On the way, the road is closed, forcing them to take a detour that may take longer, delaying their arrival at their destination. Appelstein urges the child to see that they are making progress despite taking longer to arrive. A student's mindset is often the most critical component of how much they will persevere; if they feel reasonably confident about eventually achieving their goal, it will go a long way to determine how hard they will try.[11]

Teach students specific strategies such as taking initiative and responsibility, defining tasks, planning, monitoring, and changing course when needed. Each of these attributes defines grit – and that is what is needed to succeed.

As a strength-based teacher, you want to tap into your students' hidden – and not so hidden – assets. Go beyond the individual and seek out assets available within the orbit of the student. Engaging parents is essential for students to apply lessons learned outside the classroom to their work in school. This goes far beyond reinforcing academic concepts and helps students internalize habits and values that will serve them well in other areas of life. It also communicates to them that the significant adults in their lives are working together and supporting each other. This reinforces the message the child is receiving. Research shows that positive teacher-parent relationships are associated with improving academic success; this effect is either enhanced or diminished by the extent of parent satisfaction with their child's school.[12]

The partnership between parent and teacher – and, ideally, the student – needs to be cultivated by the teacher. Frequent communication from the teacher to the parent acknowledging the student's positive attributes and accomplishments, rather than merely getting in touch when there is a problem, will go a long way in establishing a positive connection with parents that will ultimately benefit the student. To help enlist parents as your allies, create an inviting, welcoming environment. Do not share only negative news with parents; go out of your way to share the good news. It should go without saying that responding to parents within a reasonable timeframe when they reach out to you is critical.

Poor parent-teacher relationships can contribute to teacher burnout and anxiety. In addition, it can feel burdensome to have all the pressure and responsibility to educate a student fall solely on your shoulders.

Classroom Level Approaches

Just as including parents in the education process is essential, it is also helpful to include the child when appropriate. When we have input over what happens in our lives, it leads to feeling more in control, less anxious, and improves engagement. This goes for students as well. Having students become active participants in their learning will allow them to "buy into" the process. Students can be encouraged to take a more direct role in their learning rather than experiencing themselves as passive recipients of information expected to soak up information like a sponge. Thus, when teaching about the American Revolution, have your students create short plays about particular events, create a classroom constitution, or create a flyer inviting people to join the Boston Tea Party.

This idea does not mean letting students have *carte blanche* in calling the shots. Instead, you can allow them latitude within appropriate parameters you set. This allows them to participate in their learning while satisfying the requirements of the lesson. Set goals for what you and your students want to accomplish and encourage them to honestly assess the quality of their efforts and the work they produce. This is the start of a process that will allow students to develop insight into how they are faring in your class and take greater responsibility for their outcomes. Encouraging students to do this on a larger scale can make them much more engaged in the learning process. Moreover, these lessons will serve them well as they progress through school and life.

To foster a student's ability to assess their work and performance in your class, you can ask questions such as: "What was easy for you? What was difficult?" "Is there anything you might do differently next time?" Giving your students prompts to start the process will help them internalize ways to evaluate themselves. Another way to help a student assess their progress in your class is to ask them to keep a daily log to write down the areas where they experienced success. This can be almost anything, no matter the size of the accomplishment. At the end of the month, the student can review the success log with you. Having a concrete representation of what they did well over time can go a long way to instilling pride in their work and motivating them to do even better.

Allow students the opportunity to work with their peers. Collaboration is a wonderful way to foster interpersonal relationships and allow children to learn the arts of cooperation and negotiation with peers. In addition, children can practice brainstorming with each other, working through differences of opinion, and learning teamwork.

Another positive outcome is that students can learn to turn to each other for support rather than struggling alone. Learning to utilize available collective resources around them can expand a student's problem-solving effectiveness. A collaborative classroom approach can also facilitate creativity among students stimulating them to try out new ideas and learn to develop and pursue those that work while discarding those that do not. They are also exposed to new ideas and concepts their classmates share with them.

Further benefits can include improving student retention of learned material, fostering a positive attitude toward the subject matter, creating an environment of active exploration, and promoting greater attention to the task. Encouraging a collaborative approach among students is entirely consistent with a strength-based approach. Students learn successful cooperation and teamwork, problem-solving strategies, while enhancing their sense of self-competence. They can also develop friendships that carry into the cafeteria, onto the playground, to other classes, and even forward into the later grades.

Nor do the benefits of collaborative learning have to be limited to students. When educators pool their resources to create, design, and carry out learning strategies and other interventions, students and teachers win. Research shows that one effect of teacher collaboration is a demonstrable increase in students' reading and math achievement levels.[13,14]

Checking in with your class is essential. When I was a graduate psychology student, one of my placements was at an inpatient psychiatric hospital. Twice weekly, patients and staff would convene for a community meeting. The purpose of the meeting was to allow staff to take the patients' emotional pulse and allow an exchange of ideas between the residents and staff to iron out any areas of concern and keep the lines of communication open. A significant benefit for the patients was that this allowed them to be heard and have their opinions taken seriously. In addition, it helped maintain patient morale.

There is no reason why the same concept cannot be implemented in the classroom. Providing an opportunity for you and your students to check-in and address concerns can prevent issues from mushrooming into significant problems and facilitate a connection between you and your class. Addressing concerns collaboratively can help foster a sense of initiative and belonging in students. Such feelings are difficult to engender when teachers take on the role of an authority figure issuing decrees to students who have no choice but to sit passively in their seats, listen, and obey.

The classroom meeting allows everyone to express their opinions, exchange ideas, and solve problems mutually and respectfully. This may take as little as 20 to 30 minutes a week, a small expenditure of time for a potentially positive outcome. A class is a family, and encouraging an open exchange of ideas assures that each member has an opportunity to be a part of that family and take responsibility for addressing any potential problems. When children feel they are making an essential contribution to their world, their motivation and sense of control can significantly increase.

Holding community meetings communicates that the class can mobilize to act if a problem develops. Everyone is allowed to have input and some measure of responsibility regarding the situation, but classroom meetings are not a way to call out students for their transgressions. Instead, they allow students to play a meaningful role in working through classroom issues. Classroom meetings also allow students to listen to others and share ideas honestly, fostering greater class cohesiveness. Students can be given a significant degree of latitude to introduce topics within reason and always within the bounds of polite and respectful behavior toward their classmates and the teacher. Children can reason and reflect on their actions, think about the consequences of their behavior, and comprehend their impact on others and their classroom community. The teacher can establish a suggestion box, so if there are no pressing issues, suggestions can be pulled out of the box and discussed by the students at the meeting.

How the classroom community is structured impacts how the students learn and how comfortable they feel, revealing their capabilities and vulnerabilities. Classes with authority-based hierarchies can inhibit some students from taking risks and exposing what they perceive to be their deficiencies. This is not to minimize the need for rules and structure. On the contrary, such elements are critical for students to learn effectively.

An alternative approach is to view your class as a community that values positive peer relationships, humor, and respect for individual differences. These variables are effective in building students' resilience. Relational teaching is based on a perspective that values the connection between teacher and student as the bedrock of successful learning. This type of environment increases feelings of safety and confidence in being heard. The tone of the classroom environment is a variable that may be hard to quantify but has a considerable impact on what happens in class. Whether students feel supported and free to be themselves starts with you.

Just as parents monitor how their relationship is unfolding with their offspring, you are responsible for reading the tone and attitude of the students in your classroom. Teachers need to sense if there has been a rupture in the relationship between themselves and their students, and it is the teacher's responsibility to investigate what happened and try to repair it. Do not become defensive if students share information you may disagree with. Instead, acknowledge it and attempt to understand the rationale as to why the student may feel that way before discussing it with them.

When I went to school, it was not uncommon for teachers to lay down the law about what was allowed and not allowed in the classroom, starting right from Day One. I do not recall a mutual conversation, but rather the teacher simply making a declaration as the class sat passively and listened. While this approach was understood by the students, looking back, it seems there was a lost opportunity to form teacher-student connections.

This is not to say that teachers should abdicate their role to students. On the contrary, students need their teachers to create a safe classroom environment and structure to promote learning and emotional well-being. Indeed, there must be clear and absolute guidelines that everyone observes and are enforced uniformly and consistently.

Depending on their age, students can be considered allies in setting rules. Engaging your students in a conversation about the classroom's moral and behavioral expectations can help increase student ownership and establish their responsibility to each other. Collaborating with your students on rule formation and implementation is a powerful way to start the school year. Students can become active participants in developing the expectations of the class, improving their willingness to invest in them – and making them work.

Inviting the students to be active participants in setting some classroom rules has several additional benefits. First, students feel increasingly valued when their input is sought and considered. Allowing them to share their perspectives communicates that you think their ideas matter. This increases the likelihood that students will "buy into" the discussion, allowing them to exercise their critical thinking skills.

Second, you are modeling the value of working together for your students. Rather than students being put in the role of passive recipients of what you tell them, they can participate in a meaningful learning experience not only with you but with their peers.

Another benefit is that such an approach will help ensure your students fully understand what is expected of them. Most people learn best when actively participating in the learning process, and engaging with students around this topic will help ensure that this process occurs. In addition, brainstorming the ideas discussed will become increasingly meaningful for your students.

So, think about setting aside some time at the start of the school year to have a meaningful classroom conversation about collaboration and solicit active participation in setting rules. Your students will appreciate the message you are conveying – that their opinion matters. You will reap the benefits of your students' greater appreciation and eventual compliance with classroom expectations.

A strength-based teacher aims to empower students. It is liberating for students to have a fair and meaningful say in how their life circumstances will unfold. Allowing students to choose how they learn is one way they can feel a sense of control over their world and become more engaged in their learning.

This does not mean students should decide what they will and will not do in class. Instead, you can set parameters to allow students a degree of latitude within the boundaries you set. The nature of the choices available to students is totally up to you. They can range from minor, such as having students pick which book they can read from a prearranged selection of choices, to wider-ranging options, such as how they can best express their knowledge for assessments. This simple yet effective strategy allows students to feel more energized about their learning, take ownership of it, and feel greater pride in the finished product.

Students have different learning styles and particular strengths. Allowing them the latitude to demonstrate their mastery of required content will also give you a sense of their interests, talents, skills, and abilities, as well as a greater grasp of their creativity and problem-solving capability. Of course, before doing this, it is helpful to have a sense of your class and their ability levels to gauge how much structure you may need to provide.

As mentioned earlier, when students demonstrate intrinsic or internally driven motivation, their level of engagement and satisfaction with their effort rises. Giving students a choice helps improve intrinsic motivation. In one study, students were randomly assigned a situation where they could choose their homework assignment or another in which their homework was assigned. Not surprisingly, the students who had the choice of homework options reported higher levels of intrinsic motivation than those who did not have a choice. The students in the first group also reported feeling more capable of completing the homework and performed better on a test of the material than those in the group not allowed to choose their homework. These students perceived their teachers as fully supporting their autonomy and their level of intrinsic motivation as assessed on questionnaires.

As the authors of the study referenced above concluded:

> Providing choices may be the most concrete way for teachers to communicate to students that they view them as autonomous learners. Alternatively, not providing a choice may convey the opposite message. While we investigated the utility of choice with the specific pedagogical strategy of homework, we believe that the benefits of providing choices are likely to extend to other forms of schoolwork and other pedagogical strategies.[15]

Thus, offering students the opportunity to showcase their skills and knowledge has a tremendous upside and enhances confidence while developing the teacher/student relationship. As a bonus, offering greater freedom to students conveys your faith in them.

Start by emphasizing strengths. When I was a teenager, I took tennis lessons. Admittedly, my knowledge of the sport was nil, including how to hold the racket properly and the correct follow-through for a forehand or backhand swing. However, as my instructor sized me up – and probably wondered what he had gotten himself into – he noted that my serving motion was adequate. Rather than start by having me practice the aspects of the game that I had no grasp of whatsoever, he had me practice solely on my serve for an extended period. He started me off by focusing on something I did relatively well compared to other aspects of my game. Eventually, my desire to learn to play tennis grew along with my confidence. My intrinsic motivation awakened, helping me develop the momentum I needed to continue my lessons.

This experience follows the model of what a strength-based teacher can do. Rather than starting by addressing an area of extreme weakness, it can be far easier to begin with what your student can do well as a jumping-off point. Acknowledging a strength as a foundation to build upon can spare your students much pain, misery, frustration, and embarrassment. It can overcome their reluctance to make any effort at all and may even serve to awaken their motivation to stick with learning new material or a new skill rather than giving up – as it did in the case of my tennis lessons. Pairing a current strength with the new material to be covered can be a powerful starting point.

Educator Miriam Singer[16] points out that people often start from a negative perspective when setting goals for themselves. For instance, you might think: "I am heavy, so no more desserts," "I am financially strapped, so no more eating out," or "I procrastinate, so I will stop putting things off." Often these attempts do not succeed as they are rooted in things the person is not doing well and offer a low level of satisfaction. Instead of approaching these situations by correcting deficiencies, start from a positive place. Doing so can help provide a sense of empowerment and build success. For example, if a student has difficulty writing numbers but shows ability in building things, they can be encouraged to make numbers using pipe cleaners, clay, or even Legos.®

We all have different learning styles and preferences. Get to know your students' unique learning modality. Determine what kind of learners they are – visual, kinetic, auditory, or tactile. Starting with what comes most naturally or effortlessly helps ensure their motivation will be high – and stay high.

The BAWD (Build, Act, Write, Draw) model is a learning technique that draws upon this concept and can be used after the student is taught new material.[17] It gives students a choice to show their understanding of the material by selecting one of these modalities and can be used with equal effectiveness to demonstrate understanding of prior knowledge or newly presented information. It is beneficial for all ages and nearly all subject areas. Giving students the freedom to demonstrate their understanding of the material will enhance their retention, as well as their ability to generalize and apply it to novel situations in the future.

Before using BAWD, make students aware of guidelines – explain that this strategy only works if they are respectful of materials and other students. Describe what the acronym stands for and give them directions in the following way.

Build: use anything in the class or materials provided;
Act: create a skit with or without words, play Charades, sing a song, or dance;
Write: write an essay or a "how-to" narrative, compose a poem or song, make a list;
Draw: create an image on paper, a whiteboard, or use a virtual drawing app.

Students are then assigned to specific classroom areas for each activity to choose the aspect of BAWD they want to use. Allow sufficient time for the students to prepare before presenting their finished product to the class.

Allowing students to learn by beginning with what they know best or do well and demonstrating mastery by using those abilities leads with their strength throughout the entire learning process.

A strength-based teacher can help students become familiar with patterns of thinking that can either facilitate their learning or hinder it. Help your students understand that they can create the meaning they give to learning situations. This can make all the difference in the world as to whether they will succeed. Convey that the meaning they give to their experience determines whether they see themselves as having the resources to persevere or believe they are just not good enough to succeed. Helping them see their inner resilience can mean the difference between success and failure.

Self-perception goes a long way in determining the outcome. Self-concept in math and reading in young children plays a significant role in predicting later achievement in those subjects regardless of performance level. It is beneficial for teachers to be tuned into what students are telling themselves. The thoughts and ideas students have about their sense of competency can impact their actual level of success. Students who believe they are competent in math in the third grade are more likely to maintain this positive attitude in higher grades.[18]

Help students become aware that their inner thoughts which they may not be saying loud enough to hear, can have a huge impact on them. For example, as a child, I actively told myself I was not a capable athlete, and this message stayed with me for years. It was so embedded in my psyche that I avoided participating in sports. My self-beliefs controlled my expectation of success and, ultimately, my behavior, which prevented me from even trying to improve – and learning that I could not only become reasonably proficient at a sport but actually enjoy it!

To help make your students aware of their self-talk, that is, the messages that emanate from inside their heads, and if need be, to modify them, try the following steps as outlined by educator Kristen Tulsian.[19]

Teach them what self-talk is and how it can impact self-confidence. Normalize it by telling them that self-talk is an ongoing experience for all of us. Once students know what self-talk is, they can identify how it manifests itself within them. Then discuss with your students the things they feel they do well. Talk with them about upcoming tasks. What are their thoughts? Do those thoughts affect how they attempt to problem-solve?

Have them keep a daily log of their self-talk. What are they telling themselves? Tuning into self-talk will make it easier for students to track negative or self-defeating messages. Encourage them to note at least five instances of self-talk each day. Then, depending on their age, ask students to check their list to see if they can spot a particular pattern. For example, do they get particularly worried before math? Do they feel almost sick to their stomach before PE class? Identifying patterns is the first step to trying to corral negative self-talk.

Have your students develop a unique name for the thought, such as "Annoying Annie" or "Pesky Pete" to minimize its power over them. In addition to making this task somewhat lighthearted, giving a name to this quality helps students see that the thought does not define who they are but can be considered a separate entity from themselves. Naming the thoughts also helps students take back some of their power and control over negative self-talk.

The next step requires rephrasing the self-defeating thoughts into positive ones. By referring to their daily log, students can see their negativity and rephrase it into positive statements. For instance, if a student feels "there is no way I can do this (fill in the blank), so why even try?" they can instead try to change it into something affirming, such as: "At least if I try, I might improve." This skill needs practice, so doing it in groups will allow students to model this skill for each other.

As discussed previously, it is essential to teach students positive affirmations. Having students use self-expressions when needed promotes self-confidence. Evidence suggests that by having students repeat positive self-affirmations, their self-image improves as well as their grades.[20] Positive statements such as: "I can control how much effort I will put into this work," "I can accept help from others without feeling weak," or "There is no wrong decision" can be written on a bulletin board for the whole class or on index cards individual students can create themselves and have at their desk.

Again, the words we tell ourselves carry a great deal of weight. Helping students become aware of this is a valuable tool in the arsenal of the strength-based teacher. As Henry Ford said, "Whether you think you can, or you think you can't – you're right."[21] This is a skill that students will use for the rest of their lives in all aspects – personal, professional, self-growth, and so on. It is one of the best and longest-lasting gifts a teacher can give a student to carry with them into life.

Questions are key. During my student years, I was fortunate to have a variety of teachers who allowed me and other class members to feel free to pepper them with questions. I never felt constrained from approaching these particular teachers with any questions, and that helped me feel I could explore any facet of a topic that intrigued me. While it may not have been practical to do this in class, these teachers always left their door open for follow-up after the lesson.

Making students feel welcome to satisfy their curiosity offers a variety of benefits, including the obvious ones of further strengthening their relationship with you and having their quest for knowledge reinforced as they identify and develop areas of personal interest. It can also encourage self-reflection and improve or develop critical thinking skills.

Other outcomes of encouraging more student freedom are: allowing students to more fully engage with their work and with each other; helping students think aloud; facilitating learning through active discussion; empowering students to feel confident about their ideas, and improving speaking and listening skills. Encouraging questions improves student engagement on many levels.

School-Based Methods

Teachers do not have sole responsibility for promoting a strength-based culture. For an authentic strength-based culture to permeate an entire classroom, school, or district, it must start at the top. From the district superintendent down, the development and promotion of a strength-based culture must not just be talked about but actively implemented and maintained. Although that is a critical component, it is not enough to talk the talk. Districts have to embrace a strength-based culture as part of their DNA.

Many of the principles outlined in developing a strength-based classroom can be applied on a building-wide or district-wide level. Promoting collegial relationships among staff by inviting them to participate in decision-making is an excellent place to start. Encouraging teachers to share their expertise and input helps them feel valued and respected. Teachers and administrators should have ongoing opportunities to reflect, discuss, and make decisions together, focusing on what works, what doesn't, and how the strength-based model can be most effectively implemented.

A strength-based classroom without an overall cohesive sense of having other elements of the school community working within the same context is like having the 50 states working independently of each other with no federal government to coordinate their efforts. In unity, there is strength, and greater possibilities become available. Relying solely on teachers' intuition, skill level, and whatever knowledge they may already have or acquire on their own, while important, will lead to a disjointed and ineffective rollout of this model. Everyone has to start on a level playing field.

Additionally, opportunities for teachers to receive regular, ongoing feedback, discuss concerns, and offer suggestions for improved implementation of the model must be provided.

To truly develop and maintain an adequate strength-based district-wide community requires a thread that binds together schools, administrators, parents, and the community. Having each party working off the same page reinforces and ensures an effective partnership ensues. Just as classrooms should not be islands unto themselves within a school building, schools should not be cut off from the rest of the district, parents, and the community at large. Schools are products of their environments, and bridges need to be built to connect them to their communities.

Fostering connections amongst all relevant parties enables everyone to share their strengths. Parents can reinforce the efforts of strength-based teachers by understanding the model. As a result, they will be able to carry over classroom efforts in supportive ways at home. Indeed, the whole is greater than the sum of its parts.

School-wide goals for students have a great deal in common with parents' goals. As I have seen, even with families with significant dysfunction, there are strengths to find if you look hard enough. For many families, simply getting their child dressed, fed, and off to school on time with homework and lunch inside their backpack is itself a sign of strength. Many children can do well academically even while facing challenges at home if their family reinforces the importance of education. Most parents want their children to do well at school as much as teachers do.

Research confirms the benefits of close school/home collaboration.[22] These include improved attendance, more positive attitudes, and cooperative behavior, higher homework completion rates resulting in higher test scores, grades, and graduation rates, and eventually, greater enrollment in higher education. Studies confirm that family involvement in school contributes to positive results across the K-12 spectrum.

While these benefits are experienced directly by students, parents benefit from strength-based strategies implemented at school. These may include forming realistic expectations of their children and understanding the teacher's job and the curriculum. Parents with these understandings are more likely to help when teachers ask them to become more involved in their children's learning activities at home.[23]

Further, there are real benefits for teachers and school systems when parents have a significant level of involvement with their children's schools. These include school staff experiencing greater morale and job satisfaction, as well as improved communication and relations between parents, teachers, and administrators. Schools that welcome parent involvement have a better reputation within the school, district, and greater community.[24]

The strength-based model offers excellent benefits for the school, family, and the community. Each sector brings its unique contribution to the betterment of the student. It allows a wide array of parties beyond the borders of a particular school building to contribute meaningfully to student growth. Unity of the components of a school-wide community is a crucial feature of the model in which different perspectives are embraced and shared.

References

1. Haim, G. (2022). "Ginott Quotes." Goodreads. www.goodreads.com/author/quotes/212291.Haim_G_Ginott

2. Alberta Mentoring Partnership. "Creating Strength-Based Classrooms and Schools." https://albertamentors.ca/wp-content/uploads/2013/10/SB_for_Schools_and_Classrooms.pdf
3. Orange Frog Training. email with Shawn Achor, March 17, 2021.
4. Alberta Mentoring Partnership. No date. Creating Strength-Based Classrooms and Schools: A Practice Guide for Classrooms and Schools. https://albertamentors.ca/wp-content/uploads/2013/10/SB_for_Schools_and_Classrooms.pdf
5. Babad, E., Bernieri, F., & Rosenthal, R. (1991, Spring). "Students as judges of teachers' verbal and nonverbal behavior." *American Educational Research Journal*, 28(1), pp. 211–234. www.jstor.org/stable/1162885?seq=1
6. Ferlazzo, L. (2018, October 10). "Building relationships with students is the most important thing a teacher can do." *Education Week*. www.edweek.org/teaching-learning/opinion-response-building-relationships-with-students-is-the-most-important-thing-a-teacher-can-do/2018/10#:~:text=Building%20relationships%20with%20students%20promotes,our%20students%20that%20we%20care
7. Lam, S., Yim, P., Law, J., & Cheung, R. (2001, January). "The effects of classroom competition on achievement motivation. Project: Enhancement of Learning Motivation in Schools." www.researchgate.net/publication/234708757_The_Effects_of_Classroom_Competition_on_Achievement_Motivation
8. Amaro, M. (2022). "What does it mean to have high expectations for your students?" *The Highly Effective Teacher*. https://thehighlyeffectiveteacher.com/what-does-it-mean-to-have-high-expectations-for-your-students/arie
9. "How much time do teachers spend teaching." (2014). *Organization For Economic Co-Operation and Development*. www.oecd-ilibrary.org/education/education-at-a-glance-2014/how-much-time-do-teachers-spend-teaching_eag_highlights-2014-26-en
10. Renner, B. (2020, January 25). "Modern family: Average parent spends just 5 hours face-to-face with their kids per week." *Study Finds*. www.studyfinds.org/modern-family-average-parent-spends-just-5-hours-face-to-face-with-their-kids-per-week/
11. Appelstein, C. (2017). *No Such Thing as a Bad Kid*, 2nd ed. Soaring Wings Press.

12. Topor, D., Keane, S., Shelton, T., & Calkins, S. (2010). "Parent involvement and student academic performance: A multiple mediational analysis." *Journal Of Prevention & Intervention in the Community*, 38(3), pp. 183–197. https://doi.org/10.1080/10852352.2010.486297

13. Ruano, J., Heine, J., & Gebhardt, M. (2019, August 13). "Does teacher collaboration improve student achievement?" *Frontiers in Education*. https://doi.org/10.3389/feduc.2019.00085

14. McClure, C. (2008, September). "The benefits of teacher collaboration. District Administration." https://districtadministration.com/the-benefits-of-teacher-collaboration/

15. Patall, E., Cooper, H., & Wynn, S. (2010). "The effectiveness and relative importance of choice in the classroom." *Journal of Educational Psychology*, 102(4), pp. 896–915. https://doi.org/10.1037/a0019545

16. Singer, M. (2017). "Start with student strengths to promote learning." http://giftededucationcommunicator.com/gec-spring-2017/start-with-student-strengths-to-promote-learning/

17. Boutelier, S. & McPherson, N. (2018, November 13). "Playing to students' strengths: A framework for giving students choice in demonstrating their understanding of course content." *Edutopia*. www.edutopia.org/article/playing-students-strengths

18. Chen, I. (2017, October 26). "Kids' self-perception influences academic achievement." *The John Hopkins News-Letter*.

19. Tulsian, K. (2018). "The ultimate guide to helping students shift self-talk from a fixed mindset to a growth mindset." 2018. https://kirstenskaboodle.com/shift-negative-self-talk-to-positive-self-talk/

20. Ibid.

21. "Henry Ford Quotes" (2022). *Goodreads*. www.goodreads.com/quotes/978-whether-you-think-you-can-or-you-think-you-can-t-you-right

22. Henderson, A. & Berla, N. eds. (1994). "A new generation of evidence: The Family is critical to student achievement." A report from the National Committee for Citizens in Education. Center for Law and Education.

23. Jones-Smith, E. (2011). *Spotlighting the Strengths of Every Single Student: Why U.S. Schools Need a New Strengths-Based Approach.* Praeger.

24. Ibid.

A Final Thought

Every child deserves a champion – an adult who will never give up on them, who understands the power of connection, and insists that they become the best that they can possibly be.[1]

Rita Pierson, Teacher

The above quote by Rita Pierson resonates with an experience I had while I was in college. I had to take a statistics course required to complete a major in Psychology. I had not been a strong math student and was very concerned about how I would fare in the class. Any anxiety I was experiencing evaporated on the first day of class. The professor was a kind, older woman who immediately conveyed to the class that she wanted to see all of us do well and leave any concerns we had at the door. She told us she believed that all of us would complete the course success-fully and assured us she would provide any support we needed. It felt like I was meeting my math savior, and I allowed myself to soak up her optimism. For that entire semester, I believed in myself to an extent I had never experienced in a math class before. The professor provided an open forum for questions and demonstrated how we could learn from our mistakes. I received an A+ grade in the course. I recall feeling not only thrilled but also incredibly grateful for a teacher who was nonpunitive if we made mistakes, showing instead how to turn them into successes

DOI: 10.4324/9781003368014-9

I never realized I could achieve. It was a powerful lesson that stays with me to this day.

Having a teacher who actively works to build a relationship with their class and believes their students are capable of success is potent medicine for children and teens who do not believe in themselves. The experience allows students to see themselves and their world as having possibilities as they realize the voices in their heads telling them they "can't" are not the only ones they can listen to. They can take the risk of believing in themselves and have the courage to follow wherever that takes them. A teacher who understands these ideas provides a lifelong gift to their students – a mindset that embraces challenges and learns from failure while feeling valued. It is a gift they will be able to pass down to future generations.

My heartfelt belief in the power of teaching led me to write this book. I sincerely hope that reading it touched your mind, heart, and soul and provided you with the desire to see yourselves as dynamic agents of hope, optimism, and change for those students who need it the most. Writing this book has allowed me to reflect on the incredible responsibility entrusted to teachers. It can simultaneously be exhilarating and terrifying. However, the balancing act between those two states can empower you to be the best you can be, offering your students the ability to soar in ways they may never have imagined. Years later, your students will recall you not primarily for what you taught them, but also for how you made them feel. This sentiment is nicely expressed in the following quote by the renowned psychiatrist, Karl Menninger:

> What the teacher is, is more important than what he teaches.[2]

References

1.   https://soeonline.american.edu/blog/25-inspirational-quotes-for-teachers
2.   Ibid.

Appendix 1: Class Bullying Exercise

I am not sure how I learned about this exercise, but I heard about a teacher who used it with her elementary school class. It is a wonderful and powerful opportunity to enlighten students about the impact of bullying.

Dedicate a time to discuss bullying with the class. Ask them to take out a piece of paper and crumple it up. Throw it on the floor and stomp on it. Mess it up. They can do all that, but they may not rip it.

Then ask the students to unfold the paper and smooth it out. Ask them to pay attention to how scarred and dirty the paper is. Ask them to notice the lines that can't be smoothed out.

Ask the students to apologize, to tell the paper they were sorry for what they had done. Even though the students may say they are sorry and try to smooth out the paper, point out all the scars left on the paper. Explain that the scars are permanent – and they will never go away no matter how hard the students try to fix them.

Telling the students that this is what happens when one child bullies another will help them understand the irrevocability of the damage bullying can do. The scars remain forever.

Appendix 2: First Day Exercise

This is a wonderful first day exercise to do with your class. It probably works best with an elementary school-age population but can be easily adapted for use with older students. Items can be added or deleted based on the unique needs of the class. This "Survival Kit" is a great way to set a positive tone for the year.

Stand in front of the class and fill a bag with the items described below, taking time to explain why each item was chosen for a Survival Kit for the school year and what the items represent. If you are working with young students, you might first be certain they understand the concept of having such a kit on hand before discussing the one you are assembling for the class.

Here is a sample script for you to use. Feel free to improvise as needed to meet the needs of the class.

"Welcome to the X grade. I thought it would be helpful for us to get started by putting together a Survival Kit for class.

This bag contains items that represent what we'll need for success.

[Hold up each item in turn.]

The sticker is to remind you that this class sticks together and that we help each other.

The Starbursts candy reminds you that you are a star in this class and that everyone shines in their own way.

The toothpick reminds you to 'pick out' the good qualities in your classmates – and in yourself. Remember to 'pick out' the good qualities in the teacher, too!

The pencil is to remind you always to work hard and do your best.

The eraser is to remind you that everyone makes mistakes – and that's okay.

The Band-Aid® is to remind you that feelings get hurt easily, so be careful with your words – they can cause pain.

The Lifesaver® candy reminds you that you can go to an adult in this school for help.

The candle is to give you light when you feel burned out.

The confetti is to help you celebrate the good times.

The chocolate kiss reminds you that someone cares.

The battery is to help you keep going and going and going like the Energizer Bunny®.

The mint is to help you always have a fresh outlook.

The puzzle piece is to remind you that every child is an important part of the class.

The ribbon is to remind you that friendship ties our hearts together.

The cotton ball reminds you that our classroom is full of kind words and warm, comfortable feelings.

A bouncy ball reminds us that we can bounce back from setbacks. [You can use a small, soft ball like the kind used to play Jacks.]

An airplane is to remind us to 'fly high.' [You can use an inexpensive, lightweight balsa wood three-piece plane.]

A small egg timer hourglass is to remind us that time doesn't stand still and shouldn't be wasted."

At the end of the exercise, you can ask the students for ideas of things they would like to add to the class "Survival Kit" and let them explain why they would be helpful for class success.

As a reminder of the exercise and to keep it dynamic within the classroom, you might staple or glue the individual items in the "Survival Kit" to a dedicated section of a bulletin board, preferably at the front of the room. This would serve as a recap of all the qualities needed for success. Additional items can be suggested by students during the school year.

Having students be active participants in growing the "Survival Kit" will assure that the messages are reinforced, and the students are engaged in assessing what they need to succeed.

Appendix 3: How to Be a Good Friend Exercise

Have the students write a short paper describing what kind of friend they could be to someone in their favorite television show, movie, book, song, or even a historical figure (as a "tie-in" to social studies). The student describes how the character needed help, friendship, or advice to help solve a problem they were experiencing. They then write about the assets they possess and can offer the character in friendship that would help them. For instance, these can include loyalty for a character experiencing betrayal, companionship for one feeling loneliness, and others such as strength, encouragement, humor, or wisdom. The class can then read their essays aloud so all can learn about their unique assets.

Classes can also benefit from relating stories from familiar plots that demonstrate the way characters bring their assets to other characters and the story – the loyalty and camaraderie in *Star Wars*, for instance.

This assignment requires students to be honest and analytical about their own special qualities and to learn how valuable they can be to others. This task can force students to recognize how an asset they have can indeed help make a difference in the life of another person.

Appendix 4: A Strength-Based Questionnaire

The students are given a brief questionnaire asking the following:

♦ Name three things you do well.
♦ What do you think you know a lot about?
♦ Name at least two or three things you are really proud of.
♦ Name something that was hard to learn, but you learned to do well.
♦ What is something a younger sibling or cousin admires about you?
♦ What is something your previous teachers have praised you for doing?
♦ Name something you can teach others to do.
♦ Describe a time when you felt like giving up on something hard but didn't. What kept you going?
♦ What is something your friends like about you?
♦ What is something you get complimented on?
♦ What challenges have you overcome? What qualities allowed you to do this?
♦ What is something you would like to get even better at?

Using this questionnaire exercise with the students at the start of the school year can help teachers understand how their students see themselves. It can also help sensitize teachers about their students' assets (and possibly hidden assets) that could be incorporated into lesson planning in the future. The questionnaire can also be given periodically throughout the school year to see if a student can add a new strength or modify their answers to include newly learned strengths and assets. The final question can help a student set a goal and plan how they can utilize their current strengths to achieve it.

Appendix 5: Show and Tell of Strengths

Students are instructed to identify a talent they have and prepare a short presentation to illustrate it to others. It can be done in any medium they choose, including a diorama, PowerPoint presentation, preparing a poster, telling a short story, or acting one out as a skit. The student's strength is demonstrated while they explain to the class what it is and how they became proficient at it. The student can also share tips on how others can learn more about it (websites, books, local clubs, or classes) and try to become good at it. By providing a representation of their unique talent, it becomes alive and meaningful for the class.

This is especially adaptable and can be used with all ages and grade levels, including special needs students. Younger students are often involved with dance or music classes that lend themselves to a short presentation in class. Middle-school students are becoming proficient at skills and activities such as art, sports, and hobbies that can be shared by bringing in drawings or ceramics pieces, trophies or badges, or even photos of a big catch caught on the lake the previous summer. High school students may either have truly gained mastery at something or have branched out into areas such as volunteering at the local dog pound on Saturday afternoons or serving as a camp counselor in the summer.

Encourage the students to talk about abilities and strengths not generally known around school – the most effective "Show and Tell" presentation may well be the one given by the star athlete who shares his stamp collection with the class!

Appendix 6: Strength-Based Letter Writing

The student is asked to pick a particular strength or talent and write a letter to it, describing it and explaining how they came to acquire it. They can then cite examples of how they have used that strength and how it has added positivity to their life, closing the letter by expressing gratitude for the role it has played in their life.

Students can be broken up into small groups to share their letters and discuss their strengths.

Appendix 7: Kindness Activity

To introduce the activity to students, a discussion about the concept of kindness is held to ensure that students understand what they are being asked to do. It can be explained to the class that there is a direct connection between doing kind acts for others and feeling happy. This exercise allows students to achieve this by describing small, everyday acts of kindness toward others. It can be emphasized to the students that the goal is not to use acts of kindness as something to brag about but rather to genuinely enhance the lives of others. This can include volunteering at the local animal shelter, decorating the locker of a student who is not popular on their birthday, and visiting nursing homes to play games with the residents, or sending holiday cards to them.

The class is assigned a "kindness day," during which they are instructed to perform acts of kindness. This can be done for several weeks. Students are asked to keep a small journal to not only list the acts they engage in but also to describe how these acts make them feel. Students who dislike writing can keep a journal on their phones. This helps students learn that giving to others is a positive experience for both parties. Students can then share their journals. It should be emphasized to the students that it is enough to engage in small, simple acts such as holding a door for someone or letting someone know how much you appreciate them. Doing this will boost their self-confidence and help them identify their inner goodness.

Appendix 8: The Talk Show

For this activity, the teacher announces that the class will do a talk show, and everyone will get a chance to participate. The teacher can explain what a talk show is – and maybe even show a YouTube clip of one or two classic shows (Johnny Carson or David Letterman) so students can understand what is expected of them. The teacher assumes the role of producer or organizer of the show and picks four students. One of the students will be the host or interviewer, while the other three will be guests. The teacher makes a list of strengths or accomplishments for each guest. The student host meets with the teacher for a "production meeting." The host and teacher go over possible questions that can be used in the interview. The teacher can instruct the host to ask a student about particular strengths or talents, such as when the student was very patient or brave, and also about some things they can do well. The teacher can instruct the host to ask more general questions such as these if they cannot provide the host with specific examples. The teacher can give the student an index card with questions to ask.

After the host has been prepped, the teacher introduces the host who announces the guests to the classmates in the audience. The host then interviews each guest for approximately 2–3 minutes. The questions focus on the talents or accomplishments of the student being interviewed.

This activity allows students to focus on their unique resources while sharing them. Sometimes – and this is often the best part of the exercise – it can be something the rest of the class is unaware of, for instance, when the star athlete of the school shares their experience of being brave by overcoming fear of the dentist. A student who seems to do everything effortlessly might reveal that it took them two tries to earn a badge in scouting or pass their driver's license test. Those are great ways to actually "put a face" on strengths such as bravery or tenaciousness!

For Product Safety Concerns and Information please contact our EU
representative GPSR@taylorandfrancis.com
Taylor & Francis Verlag GmbH, Kaufingerstraße 24, 80331 München, Germany

www.ingramcontent.com/pod-product-compliance
Ingram Content Group UK Ltd.
Pitfield, Milton Keynes, MK11 3LW, UK
UKHW021431080625
459435UK00011B/236